LEVITICUS
THROUGH
DEUTERONOMY

WESLEY BIBLE STUDIES

This is a nice study for a Sunday school class, but not all that scholarly. Would be good to have a Wesley Study Bible using a revision of the King James (even call it The Revised King James Version) to avoid royalties. But use minor revisions to wording, and synonyms for key words from other translations, in parenthesis within the text. Did Wesley do a translation? If so, perhaps update it. Get his explanatory notes on the Old Testament. and see not only his ideas, but also what translation he used. Supplement with Clarke. Develop The Wesley Bible with a King James base?

wesleyan
PUBLISHING HOUSE
wphstore.com

CONTENTS

INTRODUCTION

Lessons from the Desert

Hiking across a desert is a far cry from a walk in the park. If we venture unprepared into a desert, we will quickly learn a few lessons. We will learn that an adequate supply of water is essential to desert travel. Thirst can quickly parch the throat, mouth, and lips. Proper clothing is also vital. We need to wear a broad-brimmed hat and light, protective clothing; otherwise, the scorching rays of the sun will burn our skin. It is also important to carry food that won't spoil. A jacket is also advisable for those cool nights that settle over a desert.

This study allows us to hitchhike with the Hebrews as they travel in the desert from Egypt to Canaan. As we join them, we can learn valuable lessons about God—lessons that will enrich our lives and make us a blessing to others.

OUR GOD IS HOLY

In the desert, God taught His people that He is holy, wholly separated from all uncleanness. Not a trace of sin exists in His nature. He also commands His people to be holy, for He is holy.

Knowing that our God is holy, we ought to disdain evil and cling to what is good. We can never correct the problem of sin in the world by being part of the problem. We must stand apart from the evil that pervades the culture. Holy people make lost sinners thirst for God.

OUR GOD IS MERCIFUL

The Hebrews sinned often in the desert. They proved to be a rebellious people. They rebelled against God by worshiping a golden calf, by whining about Him leading them into the desert, by complaining about His provisions for them, and by refusing to enter Canaan. And they rebelled against Moses, the leader God had given them. Yet, time after time, God showed them His mercy. He made a way for them to receive forgiveness and a covering for their sin through the sacrifices He appointed.

We experience mercy through the perfect sacrifice of Jesus' blood. Although we sin occasionally, we can confess our sins and receive forgiveness.

OUR GOD IS FAITHFUL

God did not scrap His plan to transport the Hebrews from Egypt to Canaan. Although the Hebrews were unfaithful, He remained faithful. He fulfilled His promise to lead them into a land flowing with milk and honey. In spite of our unfaithfulness, God remains faithful to His Word, and we can trust Him to fulfill every promise He has given us.

OUR GOD IS PURPOSEFUL

Why did God redeem the Hebrews from Egypt? Why did He carry them safely through the desert? Why did He go with them into Canaan? He performed all these gracious acts on their behalf because He had a grand plan for them. He would bless all nations through Israel, especially through the Messiah, Abraham's seed. Rebellious Israel deserved to die off in the desert, but God preserved the nation in order to fulfill His plan.

God has a plan for us too, and He is working out that plan. Sometimes He uses trials and discipline to make us pliable in His hands, but these tools are part of the "all things" that work together for the good He has designed for us.

So, as you hike through the desert in this book alongside Israel, study God's ways. You will see His character in His mighty acts. You will also learn about His character as you hear His declarations to Israel. Plan to emerge from the desert well equipped and well educated for the task of honoring Him in your daily life.

1

GOD'S DESIGN FOR WORSHIP

Leviticus 9:15–24

God's people can experience His presence when
they worship according to His plan.

The 2009 White House state dinner made history. Somehow an uninvited couple sneaked past Secret Service security, mingled with the invited guests, and even shook hands with the Obamas. The couple had successfully crashed the party.

The main message of Leviticus is this: God is holy and only those who approach Him in His prescribed way, the way of sacrifice, meet with Him. Every Levitical sacrifice pictured in some way the perfect sacrifice of God's Son. By His blood sacrifice, He made it possible for us to know and worship a holy God. This study will increase your awe of God's holiness and your gratitude for Jesus' sacrifice.

COMMENTARY

The book of Leviticus was first called by that title in the Septuagint (Greek) version of the Old Testament. The original Hebrew title was simply "and he called," which were the first three Hebrew words in the book. In Genesis, we find a record of beginnings, among those beginnings, the earth and its creatures, humanity, sin, and the Hebrew race, or children of Israel, who had settled in Egypt. Exodus records the deliverance of Israel from slavery in Egypt, followed by the giving of the law to Moses at Mount Sinai. Leviticus records God's instructions to Moses for proper worship and then describes the beginning of Israel's sacrificial worship.

In Leviticus, holiness is a key principle. The people were instructed: "I am the LORD your God; consecrate yourselves and be holy, because I am holy. . . . I am the LORD who brought you up out of Egypt to be your God; therefore be holy, because I am holy" (Lev. 11:44–45). God gave Moses detailed instructions for sacrificial worship with emphasis on holiness. Physical perfection was a prominent symbol for holiness. No physical defects were to be allowed in connection with worship. People had to be physically whole to participate. A person with a skin disease (leprosy) was banished from the assembly and could not return until a priest declared that person whole and a perfect animal had been sacrificed for that person. No blemished sacrifices were ever to be offered. Perfect animals were required. We now recognize that these requirements related to physical perfection were symbols foreshadowing Christ's future, perfect sacrifice.

In the first seven chapters of Leviticus, we find extended descriptions of the various sacrifices that were to be regularly offered. Chapter 8 describes the ordination of the priests, followed by a description of the initiation of sacrificial worship in chapter 9. The climax of these first nine chapters comes when "fire came out from the presence of the LORD and consumed the burnt offering and the fat portions on the altar. And when all the people saw it, they shouted for joy and fell facedown" (Lev. 9:24). Obedient worship in conformity with God's revealed plan brought His affirmation as the fire fell and consumed the sacrifice.

Aaron Took the Goat for the People's Sin Offering and Slaughtered It and Offered It (Lev. 9:15)

In Israelite worship, the sin offering was first. It is described in Leviticus 4:1–5:13 and 6:24–30. The sin offering was presented for unintentional sin committed by the "anointed priest" (4:3), by the "whole Israelite community" (4:13), by a "leader" (4:22), or by any other "member of the community" (4:27).

A bull was the offering designated for the priest, and a bull was also designated for the community. A male goat was the offering designated for a leader. And for an individual, a female goat or lamb was usually to be the offering. However, there was the provision for less costly offerings if the individual was poor (two doves or two young pigeons) or very poor (a tenth of an ephah of fine flour, about two quarts). In each case, the individual making the offering was to identify with the animal by laying his hand on its head before it was killed (4:4, 24, 29). When the offering was for the community, the elders were to lay their hands on its head (4:15). Symbolically, a perfect animal was being killed for the sin that had been committed.

The blood of the sacrifice was to be sprinkled "seven times before the LORD, in front of the curtain of the sanctuary" for the priest or the community (4:6), and also for priest and community some blood was to be placed "on the horns of the altar of fragrant incense that is before the LORD in the Tent of Meeting" (4:7). If the sacrifice was for leaders or for other community members, some of the blood was to be put "on the horns of the altar of burnt offering" (4:25, 30). With each offering the rest of the blood was to be poured out at the base of the altar of burnt offering. Blood, representing life, and unblemished offerings, representing holiness, were important elements of each sacrifice.

The person for whom the sin offering was made did not eat any of the meat, but the priest and male members of his family could cook and eat portions of the meat in a designated holy place. This was done originally in the courtyard of the Tent of Meeting and later at the temple (6:24–30).

As stated above, the sin offering was offered first. In true worship, the first step is to deal with sin, confessing and seeking forgiveness. Following confession, further steps in worship are possible.

He Brought the Burnt Offering and Offered It in the Prescribed Way (Lev. 9:16)

The burnt offering came next. It was often called the "whole burnt offering" because the whole animal was burned. This sacrifice is described in Leviticus 1 and 6:8–13. It was to be a male without defect from the herd or the flock. The offering represented the commitment of the worshiper to God. The person making the offering was "to lay his hand on the head of the burnt offering, and it will be accepted on his behalf to make atonement for him" (1:4). Then "the priests shall bring the blood and sprinkle it against the altar on all sides" (1:5). Last, "the priest is to burn all of it on the altar" (1:9). "It is a burnt offering, an offering made by fire, an aroma pleasing to the LORD" (1:9, 13, 17). Furthermore, "the fire on the altar must be kept burning; it must not go out. Every morning the priest is to add firewood and arrange the burnt offering on the fire and burn the fat of the fellowship offerings on it. The fire must be kept burning on the altar continuously; it must not go out" (6:12–13).

Burnt offerings were made daily (both morning and evening) by the priests, and the fat of the fellowship offerings was combined on the altar with them. They were a compulsory part of the daily priestly duties on behalf of the community, and on Sabbaths and feast days further burnt offerings were made. Burnt offerings were a constant symbol of the communion of God with His people, Israel.

Individuals could also make burnt offerings. For individuals, the burnt offering was a voluntary offering that declared devotion and commitment to God. In worship, the sin offering expressed confession, and, as a further step, the burnt offering expressed commitment.

He Also Brought the Grain Offering (Lev. 9:17)

Along with the burnt offering, the priest was to present a grain offering. It, too, was a voluntary expression of devotion to God showing gratitude for His provision. A portion was burned "on the altar as an aroma pleasing to the LORD. Aaron and his sons shall eat the rest of it, but it is to be eaten without yeast in a holy place; they are to eat it in the courtyard of the Tent of Meeting" (6:15–16). But, if the grain offering was a priest's, it "shall be burned completely; it must not be eaten" (6:23).

●

WORDS FROM WESLEY
Leviticus 9:17

Besides the burnt-sacrifice—Which was to be first offered every morning; for God will not have his ordinary and stated service swallowed up by extraordinary. (ENOT)

He Slaughtered the Ox and Ram as the Fellowship Offering for the People (Lev. 9:18–21)

Next came the fellowship offering, which entailed emphasis on both fellowship and peace. It is translated as the "peace offering" in the King James Version. This offering is described in Leviticus 3 and 7:11–34. Fellowship offerings could be made to express thankfulness (7:12), or they could be made as a result of a vow or as a freewill offering (7:16). The fellowship offering was the only offering of which the worshiper was permitted to eat a part. The animal could be from the herd (either male or female) or the flock (male or female, lamb or goat) as long as it was "without defect" (3:1, 6). "He is to lay his hand on the head of his offering and slaughter it at the entrance to the Tent of Meeting. Then Aaron's sons the priests shall sprinkle the blood against the altar on all sides" (3:2, 8, 13). "From the fellowship offering he is to bring a sacrifice made to the LORD by fire" (3:3, 9, 14). Designated parts were to be burned, but the meat could be eaten. If it was a thank offering, the meat was to be eaten the same day with none left till morning. If it was an offering for a vow or a freewill offering, then some could be eaten the same day and any leftovers on the next day. However, if any was left till the third day, it was to be burned up (7:15–18).

Cakes of bread were to be offered with the fellowship offering. Bread made without yeast was to be burned with the sacrifice. Bread made with yeast was to be given to the priest for him to eat (7:12–13). The priest was also given the breast and the right thigh. The priest presented the breast as a wave offering to the Lord (7:28–34), but the breast and thigh were to be food for the priest and his sons.

These were the regular offerings for Israel. Through them worship was fulfilled. The sin offering representing confession was followed by the burnt offering representing commitment, and the burnt offering was followed by the fellowship offering representing communion—peace and fellowship.

WORDS FROM WESLEY

Leviticus 9:22

Aaron lifted up his hands—Which was the usual rite of blessing. By this posture he signified both whence he expected the blessing, and his hearty desire of it for them. *And blessed them*—And this blessing was an act of his priestly office, no less than sacrificing. And herein He was a type of Christ, who came into the world to bless us, and when he was parting from His disciples, lifted up His hands and blessed them: yea, and in them His whole church, of which they were the elders and representatives. *And came down*— From the altar; whence he is said to came down, either 1. Because the altar stood upon raised ground, or 2. Because it was nearer the holy place, which was the upper end. (ENOT)

Then Aaron Lifted His Hands toward the People and Blessed Them (Lev. 9:22–24)

At the end of worship, Aaron blessed the people. The sacrifices were completed, and he "stepped down" from the altar. Aaron and the people had followed their prescribed sacrificial ritual. They could trust God to respond favorably. Aaron pronounced a benediction on the people.

Moses and Aaron then went into the Tent of Meeting. When they came out, they blessed the people; and the glory of the LORD appeared to all the people (v. 23). God's glory had filled the Tent of Meeting when it had been completed and set up (Ex. 40:34). At that time, Moses could not enter the tent because of God's glory. But now, Moses and Aaron both went into the tent, which was filled with the presence of God. When they came out, again they blessed the people, and the glory of the Lord appeared for all to see. God was pleased with the sacrificial worship of the people, as they were led by Aaron and followed the directions God had given to Moses. God's presence was obvious to all the people.

●

WORDS FROM WESLEY
Leviticus 9:23

And Moses—Went in with Aaron to direct him, and to see him perform those parts of his office which were to be done in the holy place, about the lights, and the table of shew-bread, and the altar of incense, upon which part of the blood of the sacrifices now offered was to be sprinkled, chap. 4:7, 16. *And blessed the people*—Prayed to God for His blessing upon them . . . and particularly for His gracious acceptation of these and all succeeding sacrifices, and for His signification thereof by some extraordinary token. *And the glory of the Lord*—Either a miraculous brightness shining from the cloudy pillar, as Ex. 16:10 or a glorious and visible discovery of God's gracious presence and acceptance of the present service. (ENOT)

Then came the climax. **Fire came out from the presence of the LORD and consumed the burnt offering and the fat portions on the altar. And when all the people saw it, they shouted for joy and fell facedown** (v. 24). God's affirmation of their worship was dramatic and unmistakable.

●

WORDS FROM WESLEY

Leviticus 9:24

And there came a fire—In token of God's approbation of the priesthood now instituted, and the sacrifices offered, and consequently of others of the like nature. And this fire now given was to be carefully kept, and not suffered to go out, chap. 6:13 and therefore was carried in a peculiar vessel in their journeys in the wilderness. *From before the Lord*—Or, *from the presence of the Lord*, that is, from the place where God was in a special manner present, either from heaven or from the holy of holies. *They shouted*—As wondering at, rejoicing in, and blessing God for this gracious discovery of himself, and His favour. This also was a figure of good things to come: Thus the Spirit descended in fire upon the apostles, so ratifying their commission, as this does that of the priests. And the descent of this holy fire into our souls, to kindle in them devout affections, and such an holy zeal as burns up all unholiness, is a certain token of God's gracious acceptance. (ENOT)

Here, worship was affirmed by fire, but fire could also reveal God's displeasure. Soon fire was to come from the presence of the Lord to punish Nadab and Abihu for a presumptious offering (10:1–2). Much later, fire came from the presence of the Lord to affirm the sacrifice of Elijah on Mount Carmel (1 Kings 18:38). May we be careful to worship in such a way that God will always affirm our offerings.

DISCUSSION

It is no secret that battles rage in many churches about how to worship. Personal preference often determines where believers draw the battle lines, but God's Word offers clear guidelines for worship that honors Him.

1. What was the first offering worshipers brought to the tabernacle? Why is it inappropriate to approach God with an unclean heart?

2. What was significant about the burnt offering? What does it suggest about the kind of worship God accepts today?

3. How can you give a freewill offering to God? Why do you agree or disagree that every offering should be made without compulsion?

4. Aaron waved the fellowship offering before the Lord as an expression of the worshiper's great joy. Does your heart rejoice when you worship? What thoughts about God and His goodness to you might cause your joy to increase when you worship?

5. What may distract a worshiper from staying focused on God? How might you focus more clearly on God as you worship?

6. When have you clearly sensed God's presence in worship? What elements in worship do you think would convey a greater sense of God's presence? Why would they help?

7. Why do you agree or disagree that reverence for God needs to be more strongly emphasized today?

8. How can Christian adults teach younger generations to worship appropriately?

PRAYER

May we "fall facedown" in repentance for our sins and "shout for joy" for the forgiveness bought by the blood of Jesus Christ.

2

YOU CAN REALLY BE HOLY

Leviticus 11:4–8, 43–45; 19:1–2, 11–18; 20:7–8

A holy life is possible, but only when we trust God for
His cleansing and then observe His standard of conduct for us.

Perhaps the word *wholly* can help us grasp what it means to be holy. The basic meaning of holy is to be wholly separated unto God. This separation includes our being wholly devoted to Him, wholly distinguishable from the ungodliness that characterizes our culture, and wholly dedicated to obey His will. God instructed His people to be holy. They would encounter uncleanness and idolatry in Canaan, but they were to display holiness by loving and obeying Him wholly. This holiness would also cause them to reach out in love to their neighbor.

This study will help you to be holy in such a way that others will see you wholly belong to God.

COMMENTARY

Leviticus outlines for the Levites (the priests) the ceremonial regulations for the people of Israel. In addition to regulations concerning sacrifices and infectious skins diseases, discharges, mildews, and the like, God gave to them a host of food restrictions here in chapter 11. One of the primary responsibilities of the priests was to distinguish between what was clean and unclean (10:10; 11:47) and to teach God's people to do likewise. The food restrictions were complicated enough to force the Israelites to constantly and continually think about God's commands and to choose what was clean. Such daily practice in simple matters such as food selection would undoubtedly cause them to consider their other actions, whether they were fitting for a people in covenant relationship with a holy God, as we see in chapter 19. Although Christians are no longer subject to the ceremonial law, there is much to be learned from it. The principles never change.

Holiness Expressed through Obedience to God (Lev. 11:4–8, 43–45)

The dietary laws in 11:4–8 can be summarized as follows: Any animal that had a **split hoof** (forming two toes) and **chew the cud** (regurgitating food from the first stomach to the mouth to rechew) was considered "clean" and could be eaten by the Israelites. Deuteronomy 14:4–5 names nine such clean animals. In Leviticus 11:9–12, God explains that of all sea creatures, only those that have fins and scales are "clean." Verses 13–23 basically pronounce birds of prey as "unclean," but all other fowl as "clean" and edible.

Some consider these food restrictions as God's protection from diseases associated with "unclean" foods. But the association between cleanness and holiness was firmly established in the Israelite mind. The fivefold repetition of **it is unclean for you** (11:4–8) was a reminder that not everything was permissible for God's people. They could not simply do as they pleased. Perhaps it was to teach them self-denial or self-control, or to ensure they would not mingle with their pagan neighbors (at the very least, they would be unable to ever eat a meal together). It is no use to try to figure out why God pronounced some animals clean and others unclean. They were clean or unclean because God said so. He and He alone determines what is right and wrong, what is holy and unholy, clean and unclean. It is His standard, not ours. His thoughts and ways are higher than ours (Isa. 55:9), and we cannot lean on our own understanding (Prov. 3:5). We are not to question, but to obey.

●

WORDS FROM WESLEY

Leviticus 11:8

Ye shall not touch—Not in order to eating, as may be gathered by comparing this with Gen. 3:3. But since the fat and skins of some of the forbidden "creatures were useful, for medicinal and other good purposes, and were used by good men, it is not probable that God would have them cast away. Thus God forbad the making of images, Ex. 20 not universally, but in order to the worshiping them, as Christian interpreters agree. (ENOT)

Note that the **coney** (v. 5), or rock badger, and the **rabbit** (v. 6) do not chew the cud from a scientific standpoint, but their chewing action resembles chewing the cud. The **pig** mentioned in verse 7 is probably a reference to the wild boar, which was also considered unclean. For all the unclean animals, God commanded, **"You must not eat their meat or touch their carcasses"** (v. 8). God wanted His people to stay far away from sin. They were not to partake of it or even to touch it, lest they be defiled. In the New Testament, we're told to actually flee from sin, to get as far away from it as possible as quickly as we can (1 Cor. 6:18; 1 Tim. 6:11; 2 Tim. 2:22).

This passage on food restrictions concludes with a call to holiness in Leviticus 11:43–45. The people were not to **make** themselves **unclean** (v. 44) by eating what was forbidden. **"I am the LORD"** (v. 45) was all the reason they needed. He was their God. He had redeemed them **out of Egypt** (v. 45). They belonged to Him.

God's people were to **be holy, because** God is **holy** (vv. 44–45). The character of God's people is based on the character of God. We are a reflection of Him.

WORDS FROM WESLEY

Leviticus 11:45

Unholy, of an holy God
The people we can never be:
But sanctify us by Thy blood,
Jesus, and we Thy face shall see.
Shall bear Thy spotless image here,
And pure before Thy throne appear. (PW, vol. 9, 62)

The food restrictions were a perpetual reminder for the Israelites of the holiness of God and their responsibility to be clean before Him. They were reminded day after day that their holiness affected every area of their lives—even the food they ate.

Holiness Expressed through Love for People (Lev. 19:1–2, 11–18)

In chapter 19, we again see that the impetus for our actions is the holiness of God. Moses is commanded to **speak to the entire assembly** (v. 2). This was a message for every single person, not just the priests or religious leaders. **"Be holy because I, the LORD your God, am holy"** (v. 2). Every command given by God has at its root the holiness of God and our responsibility to reflect that holiness.

WORDS FROM WESLEY

Leviticus 19:2

Be ye holy—Separated from all the aforementioned defilements, and entirely consecrated to God and obedient to all His laws. *I am holy*—Both in my essence, and in all my laws, which are holy and just and good. (ENOT)

The list of commands in 19:11–18 are reminiscent of the Ten Commandments, though their focus is somewhat different.

These are practical expressions of holiness in relation to other people: **Do not steal. Do not lie. Do not deceive one another. Do not swear falsely** (vv. 11–12). God's people are expected to be honest in all their dealings. Notice that lying, deception, and swearing falsely are treated separately. Lying is saying what is untrue. Deception can use words that are literally true, but with the intention of misleading another. Swearing falsely implies using God's name as proof of your truthfulness when you are conscious that you are not being honest. In doing so, you **profane the name of your God** (v. 12). In essence, you impugn God's integrity and make Him to be a liar. Jesus warned us, "Do not swear at all. . . . Simply let your 'Yes' be 'Yes,' and your 'No,' 'No'; anything beyond this comes from the evil one" (Matt. 5:34, 37).

Notice in this passage that the word **neighbor** is used repeatedly (Lev. 19:13, 15–18). God's people were obligated to treat their neighbors (not just those who lived nearby, but all those with whom they came in contact) with integrity, justice, respect, and love. **Do not defraud your neighbor or rob him** (v. 13) means we are honest in our dealings, not trying to swindle others. **Do not hold back the wages of a hired man overnight** (v. 13) is a consideration especially for the poor, who were in need of daily wages.

God's people should not **curse the deaf or put a stumbling block in front of the blind** (v. 14). Although the deaf would never hear the curse and the blind would never see the stumbling block, God would. Throughout Scripture, God is concerned with the plight of the poor, and He expects us to care for them as He would. The same concern is repeated in the New Testament (see Matt. 18:6).

God continued: **Do not pervert justice** by showing **partiality** or **favoritism** (Lev. 19:15) to either the poor or the wealthy. The poor usually ended up on the short end of justice, but God considered it equally wrong to pervert justice in favor of the poor just because they're poor. Favoritism and injustice are inconsistent with holiness and are expressly forbidden (2 Chron. 19:7; Deut. 27:19; Ex. 23:3; James 2:1–9).

WORDS FROM WESLEY
Leviticus 19:17

Thou shalt not hate—As thou dost, in effect, if thou dost not rebuke him. *Thy brother*—The same as thy neighbour, that is, every man. If thy brother hath done wrong, thou shalt neither divulge it to others, nor hate him, and smother that hatred by sullen silence; nor flatter him therein, but shalt freely and in love, tell him of his fault. *And not suffer sin upon him*—Not suffer him to lie under the guilt of any sin, which thou by rebuking him, and thereby bringing him to repentance, couldst free him from. (ENOT)

Do not go about spreading slander among your people (Lev. 19:16). **Slander** is translated "gossip" in Proverbs 11:13 and 20:19 and is rendered "talebearer" in the KJV. It is malicious gossip intended to impugn another's reputation or cause harm. It is not befitting of the people of God. Certainly we are not to **do anything that endangers** a **neighbor's life** (Lev. 19:16) or to **hate your brother in your heart** (v. 17), which is the root of much of the sinful behavior prohibited in this chapter. Some, though, misinterpret correction as hatred, but often the opposite is true. For this reason, God added, **"Rebuke your neighbor frankly so you will not share in his guilt"** (v. 17). To allow a brother or sister to continue in a sin is not love at all. True love corrects and rebukes and edifies. When we refuse to warn someone of the consequences of his or her sin, we share in the guilt (see Ezek. 33:8).

This passage concludes with, **"Do not seek revenge or bear a grudge against one of your people, but love your neighbor**

as yourself" (Lev. 19:18). The admonition not to seek revenge or bear a grudge is echoed in the New Testament. Romans 12:19 and Hebrews 10:30 tell us that it is God's place to avenge, not ours. Our responsibility is to forgive, just as we have been forgiven. **Love your neighbor as yourself** (Lev. 19:18) is the summary of all the commands listed in chapter 19. It is quoted in Matthew 5:43; 19:19; 22:39; Mark 12:31; Luke 10:27; Romans 13:9; and Galatians 5:14. Jesus claimed this commandment was second only to the command to love God with all our hearts, souls, and minds. It is the principle behind the Golden Rule in Luke 6:31 and Matthew 7:12 (where it is said to sum up the Law and the Prophets). And it is the subject of Jesus' story of the good Samaritan in Luke 10:29–37. God's people are to express God's holiness. And it affects the way they treat other people. We are to be a true neighbor to everyone we meet, treating them with dignity, respect, honesty, integrity, justice, and love. We see here that God demands outward obedience, but He also expects an inward holiness and love that radiates outward toward others. In Jesus' Sermon on the Mount (Matt. 5–7), He continually pointed His disciples to the deeper meaning of all the commandments. "You have heard that it was said" do not murder or commit adultery, "but I tell you" do not hate your brother and do not look at another woman with lust. Jesus taught that the heart was the focus. But what Jesus taught was not new; His words come right from the Old Testament. Right here God teaches that we should not hate our brother **in** our **heart** and that we should **love** our **neighbor** (Lev. 19:17–18). Holiness begins in the heart, but it doesn't end there. It affects how we treat other people.

Holiness Obtained through Consecration and Divine Grace (**Lev. 20:7–8**)

God told His people, **"Consecrate yourselves and be holy....
Keep my decrees and follow them"** (vv. 7–8). There is a

tremendous amount of human responsibility involved in holiness. We must consecrate ourselves (set ourselves apart in complete devotion) and be obedient to all God's commands. But holiness isn't just about what we do. We have a part in it, but we can't accomplish by ourselves. Notice verse 8—**"I am the LORD, who makes you holy."** Here is where divine grace meets human responsibility. It is God's grace that makes us holy. We cannot be holy apart from a relationship with Him. In the end, holiness is what God accomplishes in us; and He is able to do the work in our hearts. "May God himself, the God of peace, sanctify you [make you holy] through and through. May your whole spirit, soul and body be kept blameless at the coming of our Lord Jesus Christ. The one who calls you is faithful and he will do it (1 Thess. 5:23–24).

DISCUSSION

God never calls us to do anything we cannot do. Nor does He call us to be something we cannot be. He supplies all we need to accomplish His will and to be holy.

1. The Holy Spirit came upon the church at Pentecost, and there seemed to be tongues of fire. What does fire symbolize?

2. What kind of animals did God prohibit the Israelites from eating?

3. What was God teaching His people by dividing the animal kingdom into clean and unclean groups?

4. God wanted His people to be holy—separate and different from pagans. How should Christians differ from "pagans"?

5. What do you think characterizes authentic holiness?

6. Why do you agree or disagree that unbelievers frequently profane God's holy name? Do you think believers, too, profane His name? If so, how?

7. Based on Leviticus 19, what will a holy person not do?

8. What does it mean to consecrate oneself to the Lord? How might a believer in the business world demonstrate holiness?

9. Is holiness achieved or acquired? Defend your answer.

10. How will you demonstrate personal holiness this week?

PRAYER

Father, make us holy through Your holy power.

3

FROM RITUAL TO REALITY

Leviticus 16:6–17, 20–22, 34

Christ fulfills God's promise of eternal redemption
so we are freed to serve the living God.

Don't try to withdraw funds from the shadow of a bank. If
you need to withdraw funds, go to the real source, the bank itself.
Hebrews 10:1 refers to the Old Testament law as having "a
shadow of the good things that are coming." The priesthood, the
sacrifices, and the Day of Atonement all prefigured Christ's
priestly ministry and sacrifice. On the cross, He was the Priest
who offered the perfect sacrifice for our sins, and He was the
perfect sacrifice. We do not draw our spiritual life from the
shadow of the Old Testament law, but from the reality of Christ
and His sacrifice.

This study will increase your gratitude to Jesus for dying to
take away your sin.

COMMENTARY

Leviticus 16 is pivotal to the entire book for several reasons.
It highlights the holiest day of the Jewish calendar, the Day of
Atonement. This day, known in Hebrew as *Yom Kippur*, was the
one day a year that the high priest went into the Most Holy Place
of the tabernacle. In that room rested the ark of the covenant, the
symbol of God's presence among the Israelites.

The regulations for this holy day are introduced with a
reminder that Aaron's two oldest sons died (16:1). Nadab and
Abihu were consumed after they had "offered unauthorized fire
before the LORD, contrary to his command" (10:1). Why mention

them at the beginning of chapter 16? One reason is to highlight the importance of how the priests were to approach God. Aaron was told that he could not enter the Most Holy Place whenever he desired because of God's overwhelming presence (v. 2). Coming to meet God required a proper respect even from the high priest! On this holy occasion, Aaron was to come before the Lord in simple linen clothes and bring with him five animals for the ceremony. He needed a young bull for a sin offering and a ram for a burnt offering on behalf of himself (v. 3), as well as two male goats for a sin offering and a ram for a burnt offering on behalf of the people (v. 5). With everything prepared the ritual itself could begin.

Making Atonement (Lev. 16:6–17)

The atonement ritual had several stages. Verses 6–10 highlights the three animals designated as sin offerings: the young bull and one of the male goats would be put to death as regular sin offerings, but the second male goat would **be presented alive before the LORD to be used for making atonement by sending it into the desert as a scapegoat** (v. 10). Casting lots chose the scapegoat. Exactly how the lot casting was done is not specified. What is clear is that the choice was not left to the priest, but to God. The restoration of human beings to God always begins with God.

Some translations use the term "Azazel" instead of the term "scapegoat" used by the NIV. The Hebrew term occurs only four times in the Old Testament, all in this chapter (16:8, 10 [twice], 26). There are four proposed meanings for the term. The NIV adopts the most common one: the term is formed from a combination of *'az* ("goat") and *'azel* ("to go away"). Together they mean the "goat sent away." The basic difficulty for this view is that the Hebrew introduces the term with a prefix meaning "for." The result is "for the goat sent away." But it is the goat that is sent, not something sent to the goat. Another suggestion is that the term is similar to the Arabic term *'azala*, which means "to banish or remove." The whole term then becomes "for removal." This fits the context, but some scholars have criticized it as too abstract. A third suggestion is that it comes from the word *'azazu*, meaning "rough ground" or possibly "precipice." Later Jewish tradition understood it this way. According to that tradition, the person who led the goat away was to push it off a cliff to make sure it never returned. One difficulty with this view is that the Jewish custom reflects a much later practice, not the early one described here in Leviticus. The fourth proposal is that *'azazel* should be understood as the proper name of a demon, possibly even the Devil himself, who was supposed to live in the desert regions. Thus there is one goat for the Lord and one for Azazel. Grammatically this is the simplest solution, but it raises theological difficulties. The basic objection is this: Why would the Israelites send a goat to a desert demon? Certainly God would not command them to appease such a creature. Whatever the understanding of the term, the dramatic picture remains clear: The sins of the people are placed on the goat and removed from the community.

After a brief overview of the sin offerings, we move to more specific instructions. The first stage is the young bull offered by Aaron **to make atonement for himself and his household** (v. 11). Notice that the priest, to properly perform his job, must begin by making sure his own relationship before God is clear. In the Old Testament system, the priest was the intermediary between God and people. After offering the bull, Aaron was instructed to bring coals from the altar and two handfuls of the very best **(finely ground** [v. 12]) incense into the Most Holy Place. The burning incense would form a cloud of smoke. This smoke had a very important function: It would **conceal the atonement cover above the Testimony, so that he will not die** (v. 13). This is a clear reminder that the presence of God can be a dangerous place!

Aaron's use of the sacrificial blood dominates the next few paragraphs. He used his **finger** to **sprinkle** some **on the front of the atonement cover; then he** would **sprinkle some of it with his finger seven times before the atonement cover** (v. 14). Why does the blood of the bull need to be sprinkled eight times in total? No explicit reason is provided.

WORDS FROM WESLEY

Leviticus 16:14

Upon the mercy-seat—To teach us, that God is merciful to sinners only through and for the blood of Christ. (ENOT)

One of the goats for the sin offering is treated in a similar manner (v. 15), but this offering **would make atonement for the Most Holy Place because of the uncleanness and rebellion of the Israelites, whatever their sins** had **been** (v. 16). After the Most Holy Place, the priest would do the same for the **Tent of Meeting** (v. 16) and the sacrificial altar (v. 18). Thus atonement was offered for the entire tabernacle complex.

WORDS FROM WESLEY

Leviticus 16:16

Because of the uncleannesses of Israel—For though the people did not enter into that place, yet their sins entered thither, and would hinder the effects of the high-priest's mediation on their behalf, if God was not reconciled to them. *In the midst of their uncleanness*— In the midst of a sinful people, who defile not themselves only, but also God's sanctuary. And God hereby shewed them, how much their hearts needed to be purified, when even the tabernacle, only by standing in the midst of them, needed this expiation. (ENOT)

But how can places be atoned for? To answer the first part of this question we must remember that this chapter comes immediately after a lengthy discussion of clean and unclean (Lev. 11–15). Mildew can render unclean both clothing (13:47–59) and buildings (14:33–57). For the Israelites, uncleanness was not simply a characteristic of a moral realm. It could affect material objects. Because the tabernacle was in the middle of the camp, it too could be affected by the people's sin. Just as the priests needed to be cleansed, so did the tabernacle. The second part of the question concerns the word *atonement*. We have often used it, but spend little time defining it.

The English word *atonement* comes from a combination of Latin *adunare*, "to unite," and partly from the later English *one-ment*, "unification." Thus the adage that *atone* means to be "at one" is quite accurate. Theologically, atonement refers to restoration with God. However, in the context of this chapter, restoration is the result, but the Hebrew term *kippur* refers more to the process. In other words, what is it about these rituals that makes restoration possible? The simplest answer is found later in this chapter: "On this day atonement will be made for you, to cleanse you" (16:30). It is because of **uncleanness and rebellion** (v. 16) that atonement was necessary.

The process on this Day of Atonement started with the blood of the sin offering. The classic text can be found in these instructions: "For the life of a creature is in the blood, and I have given it to you to make atonement for yourselves on the altar; it is the blood that makes atonement for one's life" (17:11). This understanding is not confined to the Old Testament, but is reinforced in the New Testament: "without the shedding of blood there is no forgiveness" (Heb. 9:22). The giving of life is what makes restoration possible.

So far on this Day of Atonement, we have seen two sin offerings. We now turn to the quite different fate of the second goat.

Sending Away the Scapegoat (Lev. 16:20–22)

The second male goat was introduced as a sin offering (v. 5), but it was not killed nor was its blood sprinkled on sacred articles. For regular sin offerings, only one hand is placed on the animal to be sacrificed (Lev. 4:4, 24, 29, 33). The priest placed **both hands** on the scapegoat (16:21). He was then to **confess over it all the wickedness and rebellion of the Israelites—all their sins—and put them on the goat's head** (v. 21). The three terms used— **wickedness, rebellion,** and **sins**—highlight that all offenses are dealt with on this day. Rebellion covers even willful transgressions, not just unplanned actions. On the Day of Atonement, no sin was excluded!

WORDS FROM WESLEY

Leviticus 16:21

"Aaron is commanded to put the iniquities of Israel upon the scape-goat (Lev. 16:21); and this goat is said to bear the iniquities of the people (v. 22). This was plainly an imputation. Yet it could not possibly be an imputation of anything done by the animal itself. The effects also which took place upon the execution of the ordinance indicate a translation of guilt; for the congregation was cleansed, but the goat was polluted: The congregation so cleansed, that their iniquities were borne away, and to be found no more; the goat so polluted that it communicated defilement to the person who conducted it into a land not inhabited" (quoted approvingly from *Theron and Aspasio*). (WJW, vol. 9, 315)

The use of both hands and the confession of sins highlight the transference of the sin to the live goat. Once the conveyance takes place, the priest **shall send the goat away into the desert in the care of a man appointed for the task. The goat will carry on itself all their sins to a solitary place; and the man shall release it in the desert** (vv. 21–22). What clearer picture of removal is possible?

Lasting Ritual (Lev. 16:34)

The Day of Atonement was to be observed every year on the tenth day of the seventh month (v. 29). In today's calendar, it falls between late September and early October. It was not a feast day, but "a sabbath of rest, and you must deny yourselves" (v. 31). It reminded the Israelites that sin separates from God and must be dealt with. God provided a means of dealing with it, but this day—which might be viewed as a clearinghouse for all the sins of the year—was temporary. The New Testament provides God's permanent response to sin.

WORDS FROM WESLEY

Leviticus 16:34

This shall be an everlasting statute—By which were typified the two great gospel privileges; remission of sins, and access to God, both which we owe to the mediation of the Lord Jesus. (ENOT)

DISCUSSION

It has been said the New Testament is in the Old concealed; the Old Testament is in the New revealed. Old Testament glimpses of God's plan of redemption become clear in the New Testament.

1. Why did Aaron offer a bull for a sin offering?

2. Who gave the instructions for observing Yom Kippur, the Day of Atonement?

3. Why is it significant that Christ is referred to in Romans 3:25 as "a sacrifice of atonement"?

4. The Israelites were required to observe the Day of Atonement annually. Why wasn't the observance of one Day of Atonement sufficient for all time?

5. How did the scapegoat on the Day of Atonement picture Jesus' death on the cross?

6. How can you offer appropriate thanks to God for His generous forgiveness?

7. Christ is the believer's great High Priest. How does He minister to you in this role?

8. Do you see any value in elaborate rituals? Why or why not?

9. How would you counsel someone who hoped to receive forgiveness of sin by performing rituals?

PRAYER

Jesus, thank You for Your sacrifice to make us one with You, the Father, and the Spirit.

4

GOD'S WILL IN HUMAN SEXUALITY

Leviticus 18:1–6, 29–30; Numbers 5:1–7

God challenges all people to be pure in their relationships.

God wanted the Hebrews to be holy in their sexuality as well as in all of life's relationships, so He provided laws governing sexuality. In Canaan, they would encounter extremely immoral pagans. They needed to remain separate from the wicked sexual practices of the pagans.

This study will strengthen your resolve to be pure.

COMMENTARY

The book of Leviticus is often one of the most difficult for the modern-day Christian to grasp. The seemingly irrelevant details of the sacrificial system, the archaic food restrictions, and regulations concerning infectious skin diseases, mildews, and discharges cause most of us to raise our hands in surrender.

But if we look closely, we find the message of Leviticus to be timeless and deeply meaningful. It is a message of holiness and purity, a message needed as badly today as at any other time in history.

The Command: Don't Conform to the World (Lev. 18:1–6, 30)

The instructions in Leviticus 18:1–6 are what **the LORD said to Moses** (v. 1). As a newly freed people, the entire nation of Israel needed to understand God's expectations. They were free from slavery in Egypt, but they weren't free to do whatever they pleased.

Interestingly, chapter 18 is written in the standard form of an ancient covenant treaty (as is the entire book of Deuteronomy), a literary form the Israelites would have readily recognized. By framing these regulations in this way, God was emphasizing His unique relationship with them. He had promised to be their God and to bless them (Gen. 17:1–8), but only if they fulfilled their portion of the covenant. They had an obligation to "walk before [God] and be blameless" (Gen. 17:1).

God reminded them of this relationship when He told them repeatedly, **"I am the LORD your God"** (Lev. 18:2, 4–6, 30), using the covenant name for God (LORD, or *Yahweh*). In fact, in chapters 18–26, He says, "I am the LORD" forty-seven times. His name is the authority behind these instructions. As their Lord and God, He has a right to expect unquestioned obedience to His commands. He has kept His part of the covenant by delivering them from bondage in Egypt and providing for their sustenance and protection. Now it was their turn. What follows are not merely suggestions; they are commands stemming from God's person and character.

WORDS FROM WESLEY

Leviticus 18:2

Your God—Your sovereign, and lawgiver. This is often repeated because the things here forbidden were practiced and allowed by the gentiles, to whose custom He opposes divine authority and their obligation to obey His commands. (ENOT)

The prohibitions in Leviticus 18 seem obvious to most of us. The Israelites were forbidden from having sexual relationships with close relatives, with those of the same gender (v. 22), or with animals (v. 23). The key to understanding these prohibitions is found in verse 3—**You must not do as they do in Egypt,**

where you used to live, and you must not do as they do in the land of Canaan, where I am bringing you. Do not follow their practices. As revolting and unthinkable as these practices are to us—and would have been to the Israelites—they were common and accepted in Egypt and Canaan. The danger for the children of Israel was that they would become desensitized to the sinfulness around them and eventually conform to the prevailing culture. God wanted them to know that they were to be different from their culture. And so it is with us. The apostle Paul warned, "Do not conform any longer to the pattern of this world, but be transformed by the renewing of your mind" (Rom. 12:2).

WORDS FROM WESLEY
Leviticus 18:5

He shall live in them—Not only happily here, but eternally hereafter. This is added as a powerful argument why they should follow God's commands, rather than men's examples, because their life and happiness depend upon it. And though in strictness, and according to the covenant of works they could not challenge life for so doing, except their obedience was universal, perfect, constant and perpetual, and therefore no man since the fall could be justified by the law, yet by the covenant of grace this life is promised to all that obey God's commands sincerely. (ENOT)

Leviticus 18:6 serves as a summary statement of what follows: **No one is to approach any close relative** [literally, "flesh of his flesh"] **to have sexual relations** [literally, "uncover the nakedness of," a euphemism for sexual relations]. **I am the LORD.** In what follows, God made no distinction between blood relatives and those who were related through marriage. The sanctity and harmony of the family are in view here, which is impossible without sexual purity among relatives. The family was a sacred institution, and the regulations that followed were an attempt to guard it and to prevent it from becoming corrupt and defiled.

God let them know that if they chose to act as the pagan nations around them, they would suffer the same fate: "Do not defile yourselves in any of these ways, because this is how the nations that I am going to drive out before you became defiled. Even the land was defiled; so I punished it for its sin, and the land vomited out its inhabitants" (vv. 24–25). In contrast, God's people were to **obey** His **laws and be careful to follow** His **decrees** (v. 4) and to **keep** His **decrees and laws** (v. 5). The command is repeated in verse 30: **"Keep my requirements and do not follow any of the detestable customs that were practiced before you came and do not defile yourselves with them. I am the** LORD **your God."** Following the perversion of the culture actually defiles us; it makes us impure, filthy, and unfit for service to a holy God. And the entire nation would be punished for the perversion of individuals, just as God was vomiting out the Canaanites for their defilement. God's people were to be different; they were to reflect God's character.

Contemporary culture always protests that sin is fun and exciting, that one isn't truly living until he or she has indulged the sensual appetites. But exactly the opposite is true. God promises that **the man who obeys them** (His commands) **will live by them** (v. 5). That is, the obedient follower will experience true, lasting, abundant life, filled with the blessing of God. Jesus put it this way: "The thief comes only to steal and kill and destroy; I have come that they may have life, and have it to the full" (John 10:10). Leviticus 18:5 might also convey the notion that obedience is more than just outward conformity to a command; it is a continuous lifestyle that stems from a relationship with God.

The Consequence: Cut off from the Presence of God
(Lev. 18:29; Num. 5:1–7)

In Leviticus 18:29, God is clear about the consequence for sexual impurity: **Everyone who does any of these detestable things—such persons must be cut off from their people**. Excommunication was required for direct disobedience of God's commands. Such defiance, if left unchecked, would quickly defile the entire nation. The only "cure" was to remove them from the presence of God's holy people, which also effectively removed them from the blessing and presence of God. Deliberate, defiant sin was a repudiation of one's covenant relationship with God. In effect, the sinner was "thumbing his nose" at God and treating God's covenant with contempt. And God had no patience for that. Such a person had no right to receive the blessing that belonged to His covenant people. This concept carries forward into the New Testament. In addressing a problem in the Corinthian church, where a professed believer was defiantly sinning against the Lord, Paul commanded: "Expel the wicked man from among you" (1 Cor. 5:13). He told the Thessalonian Christians, "In the name of the Lord Jesus Christ, we command you, brothers, to keep away from every brother who is idle and does not live according to the teaching you received from us" (2 Thess. 3:6). Jesus himself said if a man sins and refuses to repent, "treat him as you would a pagan or a tax collector" (Matt. 18:17). The writer of Hebrews warns us even more sternly: "If we deliberately keep on sinning after we have received the knowledge of the truth, no sacrifice for sins is left, but only a fearful expectation of judgment and of raging fire that will consume the enemies of God" (Heb. 10:26–27).

WORDS FROM WESLEY

Leviticus 18:29

Cut off—This phrase therefore of cutting off, is to be understood variously, either of ecclesiastical, or civil punishment, according to the differing natures of the offences for which it is inflicted. (ENOT)

Numbers 5:1–7 describes the consequence for those who were "unclean" by no real fault of their own. Those who were afflicted with **an infectious skin disease**, which was noticeable to all; those who had **a discharge of any kind**, which generally issued from the sexual organs and, though private, could be readily verified; and those who had touched **a dead body**, causing them to be defiled but which could easily remain undetected by others, all shared the same fate: they were temporarily cut off from the people of God (v. 2). The Israelites were to **send them** away from **the camp** (v. 3). Part of God's rationale might have been to quarantine those with diseases (or exposed to diseases) that could be infectious, thereby protecting His people. But there was a bigger concept being taught here. Being physically unclean was a metaphor for spiritual uncleanness. This was God's way of teaching His people to see uncleanness of any kind as He saw it. It could not exist in the presence of a holy and pure God, **where I dwell among them** (v. 3). Allowing anything impure in the camp was offensive to God and to His holy character. The intentions of the offenders are not in question here; impurity is. Any who were considered impure had to be sent **outside the camp** (vv. 3–4), lest the entire nation be defiled by the impurity of any individual. **The Israelites did this. . . . They did just as the Lord had instructed Moses** (v. 4). Their obedience to God's command is noteworthy.

In verses 5 and 6, God shares regulations for sin in the camp that affects another individual. Sinning against another person is tantamount to being **unfaithful to the LORD** (v. 6). In reality, all sin is an affront to God. When Joseph was tempted by Potiphar's wife, he exclaimed, "How then could I do such a wicked thing and sin *against God?*" (Gen. 39:9, emphasis added). In Matthew 25:34–46, Jesus taught that what we do for others, we actually do for Him; and what we fail to do for them, we fail to do for Him.

●

WORDS FROM WESLEY

Numbers 5:7

They shall confess their sin—They shall not continue in the denial of the fact, but give glory to God, and take shame to themselves by acknowledging it. *The principal*—That is, the thing he took away, or what is equivalent to it. *And add*—Both as a compensation to the injured person for the want of his goods so long, and as a penalty upon the injurious dealer, to discourage others from such attempts. (ENOT)

Not only **must** he **confess the sin he has committed** (to the Lord and also to the individual who was wronged), he also **must make full restitution for his wrong, add one fifth to it and give it all to the person he has wronged** (Num. 5:7). It's not enough to simply confess. Things need to be made right. Full restitution of any loss resulting from the offender's actions plus a penalty of 20 percent was required. In the New Testament, Zacchaeus recognized his need to make restitution when he said, "If I have cheated anybody out of anything, I will pay back four times the amount" (Luke 19:8). Restitution served to humble the offender, to ensure no repeat of the offense, and to restore the relationship between the offender and the offended.

In Numbers 5, God mentions twice that these requirements applied both to men and women (vv. 3, 6). God does not show favoritism (Acts 10:34); His regulations apply to everyone and so do His consequences. God wanted His people to reflect His holiness and purity. From their dietary restrictions to mildews growing in their homes, from bodily discharges and infectious diseases to their sexual relationships—every aspect of their lives was to be dictated by purity and cleanness. In this respect, they were completely set apart (the meaning of the words *holy* and *sanctified*) from the nations around them. They were in covenant with a holy God. And their lives would reflect that, or they would cease to be His. The same is true for us today. We, too, are called to be holy and pure: "It is God's will that you should be sanctified: that you should avoid sexual immorality; that each of you should learn to control his own body in a way that is holy and honorable. . . . For God did not call us to be impure, but to live a holy life" (1 Thess. 4:3–4, 7).

DISCUSSION

The culture proclaims tolerance and acceptance as virtues. Anyone who insists sexual conduct must fall within biblical guidelines is labeled as prejudiced. Should believers yield to the culture or adhere to the Bible?

1. How do you know from these verses that God's commands are black and white and not gray?

2. What immoral behavior characterized Egypt and Canaan?

3. How does an immoral relationship affect a believer's relationship with God?

4. Why do you agree or disagree that attending R-rated movies or watching immoral TV shows damages one's relationship with God?

5. Why did Israel need to maintain its purity and distance from sin?

6. How should a church respond to an unmarried couple living together who requests membership?

7. Is it possible to show Christian love to homosexuals while detesting the sin of homosexuality? If so, how?

8. Is it a good idea for churches to hold sex education classes? Why or why not?

PRAYER

Father, may we live in the world without the world living in us.

5

JOY IN OBEYING GOD

Leviticus 26:3–20

God promises definite blessings of joy
to those who faithfully obey Him.

Is God a mean tyrant who stands over us, poised to zap us if
we step even an inch out of line? Of course not! He wants our
lives to resemble a cup of overflowing joy. His commands are not
designed to make us miserable but to make us joyful. There is
joy in obeying Him, but, as someone once observed, sin makes
the cup of joy spring a leak.

Jesus linked joy and obedience. He urged His disciples to keep
His commandments so their joy would be full (John 15:10–11).
This study will challenge you to obey God so your joy may overflow.

COMMENTARY

The slavery of Egypt lay behind them. Before them lay the
Promised Land of Canaan, only a short march north. There the
land flowed with milk and honey; there they would be free from
foreign domination. Most importantly, in Canaan, they would
carry out God's remarkable plan of redemption.

Before the Israelites were able to fulfill their role, God had
another "exodus" to perform. True freedom required not only
liberation from the land of slavery, but also from the mind-set
of slavery. They could not carry out their role unless they understood
who they really were as God's covenant people.

God liberated them and gave them a new identity, by "the
decrees, the laws and the regulations that the LORD established
on Mount Sinai between himself and the Israelites through

Moses" (Lev. 26:46). No longer slaves, the Israelites were now God's covenant partners. God chose to articulate this law in the well-known form of a covenant, a legal agreement between two parties. Such covenants usually began with an introduction followed by a brief summary of the relationship between the parties. Then came the obligations of the parties, followed by a statement explaining where the covenant documents would be stored and a list of witnesses to the agreement.

The final section of a covenant, nicely illustrated in Leviticus 26, is a statement of the blessings that would follow obedience and the curses that would fall on the disobedient. This chapter opens with two verses that specify certain commands the Israelites must obey.

Promised Blessings for Obedience (Lev. 26:3–13)

This section begins with an "if" clause; God's blessings depend on Israel's obedience. They must know God's commands, remember them. This is what God meant by **"If you follow my decrees and are careful to obey my commands"** (v. 3).

Given the people's proper behavior, a variety of blessings would flow abundantly. Verses 4–5 describe agricultural prosperity and a promise of rain **in its season** (v. 4), that is, at the proper time. Biblical Israel depended heavily on rain, but heavier rain was needed in late fall to nourish the freshly planted seed, while spring rains must be lighter for the crops to grow to their full potential.

WORDS FROM WESLEY

Leviticus 26:4

Rain—Therefore God placed them not in a land where there were such rivers as the Nile, to water it and make it fruitful, but in a land which depended wholly upon the rain of heaven, the key whereof God kept in His own hand, that so He might the more effectually oblige them to obedience, in which their happiness consisted. (ENOT)

With abundant, well-timed rain, Israel would have such bountiful harvests that the people would eat to their hearts' content (v. 5), for they had a binding agreement with the Creator and Sustainer of the universe.

Obedience would also bring security (vv. 6–8). With God's blessing, Israel won't fear people, wild animals, or **sword** (v. 6), that is, warfare. With Israel's location on the land bridge connecting the continents of Asia and Africa, they frequently witnessed the "passing through" of enemy armies. When they had to face battle, the obedient Israelites would experience incredible success (vv. 7–8): five would chase one hundred, and one hundred would chase ten thousand!

Using four different verbs in verse 9, God guaranteed prosperity to His obedient people. Verse 10 describes an astounding scene: The harvest would be too great to consume in one year; the old would have to be moved out to make room for the new.

WORDS FROM WESLEY

Leviticus 26:9

Establish my covenant—That is, actually perform all that I have promised in my covenant made with you. (ENOT)

God saved the best blessing for last. If the Israelites would obey, God would come, live among them, and not hate them (vv. 11–13). This last phrase sounds out of place; why would God even mention hating them? It prepares us for what we see later (especially vv. 15, 30, 43–44): Israel's disobedience and God's response. The Hebrew word translated **abhor** (v. 11) implies a loathing that has already made up its mind to reject what offends. When later verses speak of Israel abhorring God's laws, the implication is Israel hated the laws so much they rejected them and refused to comply. God's promise to **not abhor** Israel (v. 11) was a promise to not reject them.

God will link himself with His people in an especially close relationship (v. 12). He will **walk among** (v. 12) them as He did in the garden of Eden (see Gen. 3:8). God will be part of their daily lives. He seals this promise in Leviticus 26:12: **"I will ... be your God, and you will be my people."**

●

WORDS FROM WESLEY
Leviticus 26:12

I will walk among you—As I have hitherto done, both by my pillar of cloud and fire, and by my tabernacle, which have walked or gone along with you in all your journeys, and staid among you in all your stations, to protect, conduct, instruct, and comfort you. And I will own you for that peculiar people which I have singled out of mankind, to bless you here and to save you hereafter. (ENOT)

God included verse 13 for at least two reasons. First, it demonstrates how much He cared about Israel by liberating them from slavery in Egypt. The **bars of** a **yoke** were the heavy pieces of wood placed on the animal's back. No longer yoked, God's people could walk erect, with dignity and righteousness. This verse also explains, however, why the Israelites must obey. They owed it to God as the price of their liberation. For much the same reason, the Ten Commandments begin with a reminder of God's liberation (Ex. 20:2).

Threatened Disaster for Disobedience (Lev. 26:14–20)

God then told the Israelites what would happen if they disobeyed (vv. 14–39). Unlike the blessings spread out, feast-like, before the Israelites, the curses would come in waves. If the Israelites did not learn from one wave of disaster, another more serious wave would follow. The section on curses is much longer and more detailed than the blessings, as is customary in ancient legal texts. A long list of curses emphasizes their disciplinary purpose: God was giving them many opportunities to repent. It also points out how serious it is to violate a covenant with God.

God threatened with five waves of curses. He warned in the first (vv. 14–17) of plagues and military defeat. The curse opens with phrases that describe Israel's failure to obey (vv. 14–15), as if to emphasize the serious mistake they would be making. Israel stood at a crossroads: one way led to obedience and blessing, the other to disobedience and disaster.

If they violated this covenant, God himself would bring about **sudden terror, wasting diseases and fever that will destroy your sight and drain away your life** (v. 16). Crops would grow, but be eaten by Israel's enemies. Worse still, whereas God had promised He would look on them with favor (v. 9), here He promised to **set** His **face against** them (v. 17).

●

WORDS FROM WESLEY
Leviticus 26:19

The pride of your power—That is, your strength of which you are proud, your numerous and united forces, your kingdom, yea, your ark and sanctuary. *I will make your heaven as iron*—The heavens shall yield you no rain, nor the earth fruits. (ENOT)

The second curse (vv. 18–20), sent only if they did not heed the warning of the first, would be seven times worse and the polar opposite to the blessing of verse 4. Their pride became the target of His anger (v. 19). Their hard hearts led to the hardening of the sky and ground.

An invasion of wild animals was threatened in the third curse (vv. 21–22). Again, God would ratchet up by seven times the punishment to come, but only to produce repentance. Note the emphasis on motive: their continuing hostility toward God and refusal to listen to Him (v. 21). God had promised to walk among them in fellowship (v. 12), but they respond by (literally) "walking with . . . [God] in hostility" (see 2 Kings 17:25–26).

The fourth curse threatens war, plagues, and famine (Lev. 26:23–26). That God's goal is discipline, not annihilation, is clear from verses 23–24, where He described the curses as meant for "correction." The sword will come and they will retreat to their cities for protection, only to be attacked by an unseen enemy, the plague. Defeat will "avenge the breaking of the covenant" (v. 25).

Refusal to repent leads to the fifth and final curse (vv. 27–39), including cannibalism, devastation of the land, and finally, deportation. Details of their disobedience are revealed here (vv. 30, 35). Even while they had been worshiping idols, they had been offering sacrifices to God (v. 31). But God would not be fooled. He would "abhor" them (v. 30). Their cities, sanctuaries, and entire land would be so ruined even the occupying enemy would be appalled (vv. 31–33). God himself would chase them into exile (v. 33). The land, emptied of its covenant-breaking inhabitants, would enjoy its overdue sabbaths (v. 34, see v. 2).

A few people would remain in the land (vv. 36–39), but they would be so frightened that the sound of a rustling leaf would send them scampering. Those in exile would languish (vv. 38–39). These verses show the cumulative effect of sin. Like a toxic waste dump, where yesterday's cast-off chemicals continue to poison today's inhabitants, disobedient Israel would suffer not only for their own sins, but also from the lethal sludge of earlier sin.

There remains, however, cause for hope (vv. 40–45). If Israel would confess and repent, God would forgive even treachery and hostility against Him. Disobedience still exacts a price, but a merciful God wants and waits to restore. He promised to remember His covenant and the land (v. 42). They had broken the covenant, but God would not, for He was the Lord their God (v. 44).

The closing verse of the chapter contains the remarkable fact that God chose to commit himself to His people. Israel would experience the highs and lows of this chapter throughout its experience. When obedient, they would thrive under the smile of God. When disobedient, they would descend this spiral of catastrophe until the horror chamber of the Babylonian exile. Finally, they would return to God and find the forgiveness and restoration He promised.

DISCUSSION

Children who are taught to obey their parents and others in authority spare themselves much heartache throughout life if they comply. Obedience to God also carries benefits.

1. What is the first category of blessings promised in Leviticus 26?

2. What did God say would happen to those who chose to disobey Him?

3. How have you benefited from obeying God's Word?

4. Israel would defeat her enemies if she obeyed God's commands. Why do you agree or disagree that a nation's freedom depends to a great extent on its recognition of God and dependence on Him?

5. How are obedience to God and personal freedom connected?

6. What human characteristic lies at the root of disobedience?

7. Why do you think a believer sometimes chooses to disobey God?

8. How have you learned it is always best to obey God?

9. Jesus said His yoke is easy. How can parents teach their children that the way of obedience to God is the best way to go through life?

PRAYER

Father, may we keep You central in our lives through the good and bad times.

6

BLESSED TO BE A BLESSING

Numbers 6:22–27; Deuteronomy 28:1–14

God wants to bless His people through their obedience
as a testimony to a lost world.

God demanded obedience from His chosen people Israel because He wanted to bless them and make them a blessing to others. His purposes have not changed. Today, in response to our obedience, we will experience blessing and be channels of blessing to others.

This study will challenge you to obey God so His face will shine upon you and be gracious to you. In turn, you will be able to reflect His image and share His graciousness with others.

COMMENTARY

The passages of Scripture for this study fall in the last two books of the Pentateuch. The text from Numbers is a slice from the procedures the Lord used to prepare Israel spiritually to occupy the Promised Land. This spiritual preparation culminates in the celebration of the Passover.

The second text is part of a covenant ceremony found in Deuteronomy 27–29. It calls for half of the tribes to line up on Mount Ebal and the other half across the valley on Mount Gerizim. Then the Levites are to read the blessings caused by keeping the covenant and the curses for breaking it. All the people are to respond to each curse or blessing by saying "Amen."

The Directive (Num. 6:22–23)

The Lord said to Moses (v. 22) is a recurring refrain in these books. The people would stand at the doors of their tents and watch while Moses went out to talk to the Lord at the Tent of Meeting.

Aaron and his sons (v. 23) were chosen to make the sacrifices that would reconcile a holy God and His people. **Tell** them, **"This is how you are to bless the Israelites"** (v. 23). To bless someone is to seek God's special favor for him or her. Aaron and his sons raised their hands (Lev. 9:22) to bless the Israelites by saying the benediction to them. This is one of the unique traits of a prayer of blessing. It is addressed to the one receiving God's favor, not to the Lord.

The Prayer of Blessing (Num. 6:24–26)

Each verse of this benediction is an example of Hebrew parallelism. The second line of the verse parallels the idea of the first line. Each verse builds on the previous one, reaching a climax in the third one.

WORDS FROM WESLEY
Numbers 6:24

Bless thee—Bestow upon you all manner of blessings, temporal and spiritual. *Keep thee*—That is, continue His blessings to thee, and preserve thee in and to the use of them; keep thee from sin and its bitter effects. (ENOT)

The Lord (v. 24) is the only one who can grant these blessings. **The Lord bless you** (v. 24) is a general call for God's favor on His people. **The Lord make his face shine upon you** (v. 25) implies that God will greet His people with a smile. When the Lord's face shines on someone, he or she experiences the good things of life, is saved from his or her enemies, is restored, and is taught to obey God's law (Ps. 4:6; 31:16; 80:3, 7, 19). **The LORD . . . be gracious to you** (Num. 6:25). Grace is God's unearnable, undeserved, and unrepayable favor.

WORDS FROM WESLEY

Numbers 6:25

Shine upon thee—Alluding to the shining of the sun upon the earth, to enlighten, and warm, and renew the face of it. The Lord love thee, and make thee know that He loves thee. We cannot but be happy, if we have God's love; and we cannot but be easy, if we know that we have it. (ENOT)

The LORD turn his face toward you (v. 26), or "look you full in the face" (v. 26 MSG). It is a prayer for all of Israel to experience the close face-to-face relationship with the Lord (Ex. 33:11). **The LORD . . . give you peace** (Num. 6:26). The Hebrew word for peace is *shalom*. It means far more than the absence of trouble, violence, and war. This peace is the presence of everything we need to live as God created us to live.

WORDS FROM WESLEY

Numbers 6:26

Lift up his countenance—That is, look upon thee with a cheerful and pleasant countenance, as one that is well pleased with thee and thy services. *Peace*—Peace with God, with thy own conscience, and with all men; all prosperity is comprehended under this word. (ENOT)

Notice the way these pairs of blessings build in intensity and benefit for the Israelites. The first pair is God's favor in general and safety. The second pair is the Lord's smile and His grace.

The last pair is a face-to-face relationship with the Lord and everything we need to live as He created us to live.

The Promised Result (Num. 6:27)

So (as a result) **they will put my name on the Israelites.** God's covenant name is "Lord." This sacred name expresses His nature and is an extension of who He is into time and space. Lord means, "I am who I AM" (Ex. 3:14). God's name carries with it all of His power, authority, and holiness. When Aaron and his sons put the Lord's name on the Israelites, they proclaimed that He was their God and they were His people (Lev. 26:12; Jer. 7:23).

If You Obey (Deut. 28:1–2)

After recording the curses to be pronounced from Mount Ebal in Deuteronomy 27, Moses called the people of Israel to confirm the blessings from Mount Gerizim. The first fourteen verses of chapter 28 outline God's promised blessings for obedience.

If you fully obey (v. 1). This condition for God's blessings appears twice in this opening paragraph. It is found again in the closing paragraph of this text. Obedience to **the LORD your God** is the only condition established for receiving His blessings. The first blessing mentioned in this passage is that **the LORD your God will set you high above all the nations on earth.** How He will do that is explained in the following list of specific blessings (vv. 3–11).

If you fully obey the LORD your God and carefully follow all his commands (v. 1) points out that the obedience God calls for is complete and heartfelt. True obedience to the Lord grows out of reverential love (Deut. 10:12–13). Obedience to the Lord's commands is a result of our relationship with Him. It is the sole condition for receiving God's blessings.

All these blessings—listed in the following verses, as well as those detailed in the rest of Deuteronomy—**will come upon**

you and accompany you if you obey the LORD your God (28:2).
We should take note that these verses are addressed to "the
Israelites" (Deut. 29:1). The word *you* here is therefore plural. A
person's blessings were contingent upon the obedience of the
nation of Israel. These promised blessings are for the group and
not just the individual.

You Will Be Blessed (Deut. 28:3–8)
You will be blessed in the city and blessed in the country
(v. 3). No one will be left out. **The fruit of your womb will be
blessed** (v. 4) means you will have many healthy children. In
fact, **the crops of your land and the young of your livestock**
(v. 4) will also be plentiful. These are absolutely vital to an agricultural society. **Your basket** for collecting food will not be
empty, **and your kneading trough** for preparing the food **will
be blessed** (v. 5). You will have plenty to eat and it will taste
good to you. **You will be blessed when you come in and
blessed when you go out** (v. 6). If you obey God's commands
you will be surrounded with His blessings twenty-four hours a
day, seven days a week. There is no limit to the blessings the
Lord wants to give His people.

●

WORDS FROM WESLEY
Deuteronomy 28:3

Streams—The most dry and barren places shall be made moist
and fruitful: which is principally meant of the plentiful effusion
of God's grace upon such persons and nations, as had been wholly
destitute of it. *Rushes*—Those dry and parched deserts, in which
dragons have their abode, shall yield abundance of grass, and
reeds, and rushes, which grow only in moist ground. (ENOT)

**The LORD will grant that the enemies who rise up against
you will be defeated before you** (v. 7). Your enemies **will come**

at you from one direction but flee from you in seven (v. 7). They will be routed, defeated and dispersed by the Lord.

The Lord will send a blessing on your barns (v. 8) so they are always full of provisions for you. **The Lord will send a blessing . . . on everything you put your hand to** (v. 8). You will receive His supernatural help in every endeavor. **The LORD your God will bless you in the land he is giving you** (v. 8). The Promised Land is God's gracious gift to you and His favor will rest on you there.

You Will Be God's People (Deut. 28:9–11)

The LORD will establish you as his holy people (v. 9). This is the greatest blessing in the whole list. It is the only one that makes God's people like Him. When Israel is established as God's **holy people . . . then all the peoples on earth will see that you are called by the name of the LORD** (vv. 9–10). They will see that Israel is unique and set apart. God's people are holy because of their uncommon relationship with the Lord and because that relationship shapes their conversations and conduct. In fact, this blessing is based on the condition of obedience. A holy lifestyle of obedience to God's laws and a holy relationship to the Lord are inseparable. One cannot exist without the other.

Verses 10–11 form a bridge from the list of promised blessings to the concluding paragraph in verses 12–14. **The peoples on earth . . . will fear you** (v. 10) because they will realize you are God's holy people and that He protects you. **The LORD will grant you abundant prosperity** (v. 11). We must resist the very human tendency to equate abundant prosperity with the Lord's approval. That was the mistake Job and his comforters made when he was suffering. Prosperity without a proper relationship to the Lord is not a blessing (Prov. 15:16; 16:8). These material blessings are gifts God gives in response to the obedience of His people. They are not something His people earn with their obedience.

Obey and Be on Top (Deut. 28:12–14)

This paragraph serves as a conclusion to this section on the covenant's blessings. Verse 12 and the beginning of verse 13 provide a culminating summary of the physical blessings promised before: **The LORD will open the heavens, the storehouse of his bounty, to send rain on your land in season** (v. 12). In other words, not only will your crops receive enough rain, it will also come at the right times. God will also **bless all the work of your hands** (v. 12). Everything you attempt will succeed until you have more than you need. Then **you will lend to many nations but will borrow from none. The LORD will make you the head, not the tail** (vv. 12–13). When the Lord blesses His people they end up on top of the world.

But Moses would not let Israel think these blessings are automatic or without requirement. Just as he opened this section on blessings with a call to "obey the LORD your God" (vv. 1–2), so now he closed by repeating the same call: **If you pay attention to the commands of the LORD your God that I give you this day and carefully follow them, you will always be at the top, never at the bottom** (v. 13). And Moses stressed the kind of obedience that would bring God's blessings. Only willing, loving, complete, perfect, and total obedience would meet the conditions for the covenant blessings. **Do not turn aside from any of the commands I give you today, to the right or to the left** (v. 14). Finally, Moses reminded the people that all their obedience must grow out of a deeply loyal and exclusive relationship with the Lord their God. They must have a relationship with Him that keeps them from **following other gods and serving them** (v. 14).

DISCUSSION

"Bless you," someone may say when you sneeze. But what does it mean to be blessed? Discuss what conditions attached to God's blessings.

1. What does God's blessing include in addition to material provisions?

2. How do you explain the fact that many believers in Third-World countries have so few material possessions?

3. If you suddenly lost everything you own, would you still feel blessed? Why or why not?

4. How has God shown you that He is gracious?

5. Why would you agree that God's greatest blessing is His presence?

6. How can you share more of what God has blessed you with?

7. Why do you agree or disagree that God's blessings are not a paycheck?

8. Is a person's motive right if he or she obeys God to get something from Him? What should our motives be in obeying God?

9. What was God's ultimate purpose in blessing Israel?

10. What do you think God's ultimate purpose is in blessing Christians?

PRAYER

Father, may we bless others as You bless us.

7

CAN I REALLY TRUST GOD?

Numbers 13:1–3; 13:25—14:11

Will I trust God?

Some Christians see God and trust Him; others see giants and doubt Him. A majority report by the spies Moses sent into Canaan focused on the giants there. Joshua and Caleb brought a minority report. Yes, they, too, had seen giants, but they believed God was bigger than the giants, and they urged Israel to believe God and invade Canaan immediately.

"Giants" threaten us too. Giant problems, giant challenges, and giant attacks on our faith. We can easily feel overwhelmed and powerless if we focus on the giants instead of on God. But God is all powerful, and His promises are ironclad. This study will challenge you to trust God for victory even when you face what seem to be insurmountable odds.

COMMENTARY

The book of Numbers records the journey of Israel from Mount Sinai to the border of the Promised Land. During this trip, God led His people through both spiritual and military preparation. Unfortunately, what should have been a short, straight trek to victorious blessing became a forty-year walk around the wilderness waiting for an entire generation to die.

The military and human preparations were supposed to be the secondary emphasis even though they are the basis for the book's title. The first four chapters deal with counting and organizing the various tribes for their travels. These were done at Mount Sinai.

The spiritual preparations were intended to be the primary emphasis for the Israelites. These measures are detailed in Numbers 5–10. In chapter 5, God told Moses how the people were to get rid of uncleanness, conflict, and jealousy. In chapter 6, the Lord outlined the Nazirite vow and the priestly prayer of blessing. Chapter 7 details the dedication of the tabernacle. The Levites were consecrated and put into service in chapter 8. The Israelites celebrated the second Passover at Mount Sinai (9:1–14). Then the cloud of God's presence led them toward the Promised Land (9:15—10:36).

In spite of all these reminders of God's power, not to mention the events of Exodus, the people majored on the minors and failed to trust God. They complained about their hardships and the Lord judged them by burning the edges of their camp (Num. 11:1–4). Even though the people had seen the plagues on Egypt and had watched the Red Sea swallow the Egyptian army, they complained about the diet of manna God provided. So, the Lord sent them so much quail to eat that many of them died (11:5–35). Even the high priest Aaron and the prophetess Miriam rebelled against God's chosen leader, Moses. God nearly killed them, but Moses interceded and they were spared (ch. 12).

All these blessings and curses form the backdrop for chapters 13–14. By all appearances, these people should be ready to face any obstacle they might encounter. But looks can be deceiving.

Send Twelve Men (Num. 13:1–3)

The Lord said to Moses, "Send some men" (vv. 1–2). In Deuteronomy 1:22, Moses said the people said, "Let us send men ahead to spy out the land for us and bring back a report about the route we are to take and the towns we will come to." The idea seemed good to Moses (Deut. 1:23) and apparently to the Lord as well. So, He told Moses to **"send some men to explore the land of Canaan, which I am giving to the**

Israelites" (Num. 13:2). There does not seem to be any question on God's part as to the future of this venture. He said He would give the land to the Israelites. And in Deuteronomy, Moses didn't question the outcome. He told the people, "See, the LORD your God has given you the land. Go up and take possession of it as the LORD, the God of your fathers, told you. Do not be afraid; do not be discouraged" (Deut. 1:21). The people appeared to be planning the route they would take as they entered the land, too. **From each ancestral tribe send one of its leaders** (Num. 13:2). These men were leaders sent to explore the Promised Land and to discern the way to take possession of it. **So at the LORD's command Moses sent them out** (v. 3). It is important to note that this all happened **at the LORD's command**. Although the people suggested it and Moses thought it was a good idea, it was done because God told Moses to do it. **Moses sent them out from the Desert of Paran** (v. 3), where the people had camped at a place called Kadesh (v. 26). Kadesh must have been located on the frontier between the Desert of Paran and the Desert of Zin. **All of** the men **were leaders of the Israelites** (v. 3) and must have been very influential.

It's a Good Land But ... (Num. 13:25–29)

Numbers 13:4–24 lists the names of the twelve leaders and outlines the route they took through the Promised Land. They visited Hebron (v. 22), where the patriarchs had lived. However, instead of being reminded of the Lord's covenant with Abraham, Isaac, and Jacob, they were impressed by the size of Hebron's citizens (vv. 22–33). These men returned with "a branch bearing a single cluster of grapes . . . along with some pomegranates and figs" (v. 23). **At the end of forty days they returned from exploring the land** (v. 25).

They came back to Moses and Aaron (God's chosen leaders of leaders) **and the whole Israelite community** (v. 26). Their report included showing **them the fruit of the land**. **They gave Moses** and the people **this account: "We went into the land to which you sent us, and it does flow with milk and honey! Here is its fruit"** (vv. 26–27). This land was all God had promised (Ex. 3:17).

WORDS FROM WESLEY
Numbers 13:25

They returned after forty days— 'Tis a wonder the people had patience to stay forty days, when they were just ready to enter Canaan, under all the assurances of success they could have from the Divine power, proved by a constant series of miracles, that had hitherto attended them. But they distrusted God, and chose to be held in suspense by their own counsels, rather than to rest upon God's promise! How much do we stand in our own light by unbelief? (ENOT)

But is a powerful word. It contrasts the positive opening line with the negative ones to follow. **"But the people who live there are powerful** militarily. **The cities are fortified and very large"** (Num. 13:28). These men had seen the cities and armies of Egypt and were still impressed with what they saw in the Promised Land. **"We even saw descendants of Anak there"** (v. 28). The descendants of Anak were giants compared to the Israelites (v. 33). And there were even more people groups in the land: the **Amalekites**, **Hittites**, **Jebusites**, **Amorites**, and **Canaanites** (v. 29). God had already told them about these inhabitants (Ex. 3:8, 17; 13:5).

Caleb's Call to Arms (Num. 13:30)

This report must have caused pandemonium because **Caleb** needed to silence **the people before Moses** (v. 30) so he could speak. Caleb represented the tribe of Judah. He did not disagree with the facts of the initial report. His speech went straight to a faith-filled call to arms: **"We should go up and take possession of the land, for we can certainly do it."** Caleb was focused on the power of the Lord that brought them out of Egypt. He had no doubt as to the outcome. God can do whatever He has promised to do (Num. 14:8).

●

WORDS FROM WESLEY

Numbers 13:30

Silence, ye unbelieving fears,
Who clamorously deny the word!
The promise on our side appears,
The power and goodness of our Lord:
Let us go up in Jesu's name:
Our sins shall all to Christ submit,
And who for us the world o'ercame,
Shall bruise the fiend beneath our feet.
Is anything too hard for God?
Through Jesus we can all things do;
Who Satan and his works destroy'd,
Shall make us more than conquerors too:
Let us at once the land possess,
And taste the blessings from above,
The milk sincere of pardoning grace,
The honey of His perfect love. (PW, vol. 9, 73)

We're Like Grasshoppers (Num. 13:31–33)

But the men who had gone up with Caleb presented a doubt filled response. They **said, "We can't attack those people"** (v. 31). These men were thinking of the censuses of the tribes done at Mount Sinai. Perhaps they also realized that brick-making slaves were not trained soldiers. They went on to say, **"They are stronger than we are"** (v. 31). They were giants and the Israelites were not. So **they spread among the Israelites a bad report about the land they had explored** (v. 32). These ten leaders influenced the people to distrust God's ability to keep His promises.

They said, "The land we explored devours those living in it" (v. 32). The land is so fertile and fruitful that it always filled with conflict as others seek to control it. **"All the people we saw there are of great size. We saw the Nephilim there"** (vv. 32–33). The Nephilim are mentioned in Genesis 6:4 and must have been men of giant size and strength. Because the people were so strong and tall, **"We seemed like grasshoppers in our own eyes, and we looked the same to them"** (v. 33). Note that these men make no mention of how the Nephilim seemed to the Lord.

Wailing, Grumbling, and Going Back to Egypt (Num. 14:1–4)

That night all the people of the community (v. 1) responded to the bad report in a reasonable way—assuming it was correct. They **raised their voices and wept aloud** (v. 1). Ten of their leaders were telling them there was no hope. They felt abandoned and betrayed. So **all the Israelites grumbled against Moses and Aaron, and the whole assembly said to them, "If only we had died in Egypt! Or in this desert!"** (v. 2). This was their repeated response to difficulty (Ex. 15:24; 16:2; 17:3; Num. 16:41). They seemed to think the pain of the present was worse than death in some other situation.

The doubt-filled report of the ten leaders bred distrust in the Israelites: **Why is the LORD bringing us to this land only to let us fall by the sword?** (Num. 14:3). They not only express doubt regarding the Lord's ability to keep His promise, they question His motives and His love for them. Then they assume the worst will happen: **Our wives and children will be taken as plunder**. And if that were the case, **wouldn't it be better for us to go back to Egypt?** (v. 3). The people were suffering from a "moral dementia." They thought the ruthless slavery of Egypt would be better than God's plan for them. They lost track of the spiritual realities and experiences the Lord provided for them. **So they said to each other, "We should choose a leader and go back to Egypt"** (v. 4). Their disobedient rebellion was complete because Moses and Aaron were not the leaders who brought them out of Egypt. The Lord was their leader and they chose to replace Him.

WORDS FROM WESLEY

Numbers 14:4

A captain—Instead of Moses, one who will be more faithful to our interest than he. *Into Egypt*—Stupendous madness! Whence should they have protection against the hazards, and provision against all the wants of the wilderness? Could they expect either God's cloud to cover and guide them, or Manna from heaven to feed them? Who could conduct them over the Red Sea? Or, if they went another way, who should defend them against those nations whose borders they were to pass? What entertainment could they expect from the Egyptians, whom they had deserted and brought to so much ruin? (ENOT)

Four Faithful Men (Num. 14:5–9)

Only four men stood with God at Kadesh. **Moses and Aaron fell facedown** to pray **in front of the whole Israelite assembly gathered there. Joshua son of Nun and Caleb son of Jephunneh, who were among those who had explored the land, tore their clothes** (vv. 5–6) as an expression of grief over Israel's sin. They said, **"The land we passed through and explored is exceedingly good"** (v. 7). Again all the leaders sent to see the land agreed on this point. Then they added their reason for choosing to obey God: **"If the LORD is pleased with us, he will lead us into that land, a land flowing with milk and honey, and will give it to us"** (v. 8). Moses, Aaron, Joshua, and Caleb recognized that the real issue was the Lord's desire to bless His people.

So they said, **"Do not rebel against the LORD. And do not be afraid of the people of the land, because we will swallow them up. Their protection is gone, but the LORD is with us. Do not be afraid of them"** (v. 9). Joshua and Caleb would live to see this all become a reality but not the rest of their generation (Josh. 2:8–11).

WORDS FROM WESLEY
Numbers 14:9

Bread—We shall destroy them as easily as we eat our bread. *Their defence*—Their conduct and courage, and especially God, who was pleased to afford them His protection 'till their iniquities were full, is utterly departed from them, and hath given them up as a prey to us. *With us*—By His special grace and almighty power, to save us from them and all our enemies. *Only rebel not against the Lord*—Nothing can ruin sinners but their own rebellion. If God leaves them, 'tis because they drive Him from them, and they die, because they will die. (ENOT)

Kill Them (Num. 14:10–11)

But the whole assembly talked about stoning them (v. 10). The Israelites chose to kill the four faithful men instead of obeying God. **Then the glory of the LORD appeared at the Tent of Meeting to all the Israelites** (v. 10). God intervened to save His loyal servants. **The LORD said to Moses, "How long will these people treat me with contempt? How long will they refuse to believe in me, in spite of all the miraculous signs I have performed among them?"** (v. 11). Here is the key to understanding all sin and rebellion against God. From Adam and Eve in the garden of Eden to the Israelites at Kadesh to every other human being, humans refuse to believe in God. That distrust always leads to disobedience and judgment. The only solution for this problem is to trust the Lord enough to obey Him.

DISCUSSION

The Israelites were certainly a forgetful and rebellious people. They quickly forgot God's blessings and often refused to obey Him. Discuss how Christians today are any different.

1. What part of the Israelite spies' report of Canaan was perceived as bad news? What part was good news?

2. What bad news and good news reach believers today?

3. How can believers focus on good news when we are exposed to so much bad news?

4. How is it possible that a majority vote doesn't necessarily reflect God's will in a matter?

5. What is essential in gaining victory over the believer's enemy—big faith in a God who is perceived to be small or little faith in a God who is perceived to be big? Explain.

6. What giant-sized problems may confront Christians when they attempt to accomplish God's will?

7. What do you think is an effective cure for grumbling?

8. Why do you agree or disagree that Christians seldom rebel against the Lord?

9. What good things do you believe lie just ahead for those who trust the Lord?

PRAYER

Father, help us to look at life from Your powerful perspective, rather than our timid viewpoint.

THE DEMANDS OF LEADERSHIP

Numbers 20:1–12; Deuteronomy 3:23–29

God wants leaders to keep a cool head in spite of challenges
and frustrations, obeying Him to the very end.

A pastor received a get-well card from the church board. A
note enclosed with the card announced, "By a vote of six to five,
the board decided to send this card."

Leading a congregation is a heavy responsibility, and occasionally
a pastor's popularity may sink like a rock. He or she may be in the
right, but that is sometimes a lonely place. Occasionally, the
Hebrews rebelled against Moses' leadership, but their rebellion
was groundless, and it angered the Lord.

This study will help you see that your spiritual leaders are
human, but they deserve your support as they try to fulfill the
demands of leadership.

COMMENTARY

The book of Numbers records Israel's journey from Sinai to
the border of Canaan.

As a result of their distrust and disobedience, Israelites twenty
years of age and older were condemned to die in the wilderness.
The only exceptions were the Lord's two faithful scouts: Joshua and
Caleb (Num. 14:26–35). The whole nation's progress was halted
for "forty years—one year for each of the forty days you explored
the land" until that rebellious generation died (14:34).

Kadesh was to be the launch pad for Israel's possession of
the Promised Land. Now the entire community gathered at Kadesh
once again.

Miriam Dies in the Desert (Num. 20:1)

In the first month (v. 1) of the fortieth year of wandering (Num. 20:22–29; 33:38), **Miriam** (Moses' older sister) **died and was buried** (20:1). Miriam was a key player on God's leadership team for the Israelites. Through the prophet Micah, the Lord reminded His people, "I brought you up out of Egypt and redeemed you from the land of slavery. I sent Moses to lead you, also Aaron and Miriam" (Mic. 6:4). However, her feelings of importance led her to join Aaron in challenging Moses' leadership (Num. 12:1–15). There is no mention of Miriam in the narrative of Israel's rebellion the first time they came to Kadesh. It appears that she did not join Moses and Aaron in trying to persuade the people to obey the Lord. So, Miriam died in the desert with the rest of her generation.

No Water in the Desert (Num. 20:2–5)

Now that the all the Israelites had gathered at Kadesh, **there was no water for the community** (v. 2). Obviously, water is the greatest need in desert travel. And finding water for thousands of human beings and their livestock would be an immense problem.

●

WORDS FROM WESLEY

Numbers 20:3

Before the Lord—Suddenly, rather than to die such a lingering death. Their sin was much greater than that of their parents, because they should have taken warning by their miscarriages, and by the terrible effects of them, which their eyes had seen. (ENOT)

So when they became thirsty, **the people gathered in opposition to Moses and Aaron** (v. 2). The parents and grandparents of this new generation had done the same thing near Mount Sinai (Ex. 17:1–7). **They quarreled with Moses** (just like the previous generation) **and said, "If only we had died when our brothers fell dead before the LORD!"** (Num. 20:3). They may have been referring to the plague that killed more than fourteen thousand Israelites when they grumbled against Moses when God struck 250 rebels dead and had the ground swallow the ring leaders (Num. 16).

Again just like the previous generation, they asked, **"Why did you bring the LORD's community into this desert, that we and our livestock should die here? Why did you bring us up out of Egypt to this terrible place? It has no grain or figs, grapevines or pomegranates. And there is no water to drink!"** (20:4–5). Complaining about uncomfortable and difficult situations came easily to these people. Three days after the great worship celebration on the safe side of the Red Sea, they grumbled about being thirsty (Ex. 15:22–25). Then a few weeks later they complained about being hungry (16:1–3). The next time they were thirsty, they complained (17:1–7). When they became bored with manna, they moaned and wailed about the good food in Egypt (Num. 11:4–35). When they were scared of the giant inhabitants of the Promised Land, they grumbled and wanted to go back to Egypt (14:1–4).

The Lord's Directions (Num. 20:6–8)

Moses and Aaron did what all leaders should do in times of crisis. They **went from the assembly to the entrance to the Tent of Meeting and fell facedown, and the glory of the LORD appeared to them** (v. 6). This was Moses' consistent response to the grumbling of the Israelites. Sometimes he asked the Lord to explain why the difficulties had arisen (Ex. 5:22–6:9; Num. 11:10–25). At other times he sought the Lord's directions for what he should do next (Ex. 14:15–18; 15:25; 16:4–7; 17:4–7). On more than one occasion, Moses interceded on their behalf and asked God to spare them from His judgment (Ex. 32:9–14; Num. 11:1–3; 14:5–20; 16:22–24, 41–50).

The LORD said to Moses, "Take the staff" (20:7–8) which had been the symbol of the Lord's power starting at the burning bush in Exodus 3–4. **"You and your brother Aaron gather the assembly together"** (Num. 20:8). Previously, the Lord provided water in the sight of Israel's elders alone (Ex. 17:6). In this situation, He wanted the whole assembly to see His provision. **"Speak to that rock before their eyes and it will pour out its water"** (Num. 20:8). This command was also different from the first time where the Lord told Moses to strike the rock (Ex. 17:6). **"You will bring water out of the rock for the community so they and their livestock can drink"** (Num. 20:8). God promised to provide water just as He had before.

Moses' Actions (Num. 20:9–11)

So Moses took the staff from the LORD's presence, just as he commanded him (v. 9). This was Moses' regular response. The Lord would tell him to do something and Moses would do it. **He and Aaron gathered the assembly together in front of the rock** (v. 10).

But something happened that God had not commanded. **Moses said to** the people and not to the rock, **"Listen, you rebels, must we bring you water out of this rock?"** (v. 10). **We** may refer to Moses and Aaron alone or to Moses, Aaron, and God. **Then Moses raised his arm and struck the rock twice with his staff** (v. 11). That was not what the Lord had commanded. However, He graciously provided for His people anyway. **Water gushed out, and the community and their livestock drank** (v. 11).

No Trust Means No Trip (Num. 20:12)

But the LORD said to Moses and Aaron, "Because you did not trust in me enough to honor me as holy in the sight of the Israelites, you will not bring this community into the land I give them" (v. 12). One act of distrust and disobedience barred

Moses and Aaron from entering the land. Trust and obedience are just as important for the leaders of God's people as for the people.

The connection between distrust and disobedience first appears in Genesis 3, when the serpent entered the garden of Eden. The serpent told lies about sin and humans but mainly about God. Adam and Eve believed Satan's lies, so they distrusted God and deliberately disobeyed His command. When God confronted Adam, Eve, and the serpent, He cursed (passed judgment on) them all.

The connection between trust and obedience comes through clearly in Genesis 15, when God revealed the truth about himself to Abram. Abram trusted God because he believed Him "and he credited it to him as righteousness" (Gen. 15:6). Abram obeyed God because he believed. So, God blessed Abram and "all peoples on earth" (Gen. 12:3).

While it is possible to obey God without trusting Him, it is impossible to disobey God and trust Him at the same time. The very act of willfully transgressing the Lord's command revealed the Israelites' distrust and unbelief (Num. 27:14; Deut. 32:51). In that crucial moment, Moses and Aaron chose to trust in their own judgment. The essence of their sin was no different than that of Adam and Eve or the people who refused to enter the land (Num. 14).

WORDS FROM WESLEY
Numbers 20:12

Ye believed me not—But shewed your infidelity: which they did, either by smiting the rock, and that twice, which is emphatically noted, as if he doubted whether once smiting would have done it, whereas he was not commanded to smite so much as once, but only to speak to it. (ENOT)

The punishment for this one act of unbelief prevented Moses and Aaron from enjoying the fruit of their life mission. But sin is always like that. Even though God has forgiven the transgression, sin limits future possibilities.

Please Let Me Go (Deut. 3:23–25)

At that time I pleaded with the LORD (v. 23). Moses interceded for himself just as he had prayed for the people on other occasions. He began by recognizing God's absolute authority and His covenant relationship: **"O Sovereign LORD, you have begun to show to your servant your greatness and your strong hand"** (v. 24). The more of God Moses experienced, the more he wanted to see. **"For what god is there in heaven or on earth who can do the deeds and mighty works you do?"** (v. 24). Moses knew no one could compete with all the Lord had done for Israel. **"Let me go over and see the good land beyond the Jordan—that fine hill country and Lebanon"** (v. 25). He longed to see the whole land from the south to the north.

WORDS FROM WESLEY

Deuteronomy 3:23

I besought the Lord—We should allow no desire in our hearts, which we cannot in faith offer unto God by prayer. (ENOT)

Don't Ask Again (Deut. 3:26–29)

But because of you the LORD was angry with me (v. 26). Just as Adam and Eve blamed another for their sin, so did Moses. He repeated this litany of finger pointing twice in Deuteronomy (1:37; 3:26). **The LORD . . . would not listen to me** (v. 26). He would not grant Moses' request. **"That is enough,"** the LORD **said** (v. 26). The tone of God's answer indicates that this prayer was repeated and persistent. **"Do not speak to me anymore about this matter. Go up to the top of Pisgah and look west and north and south and east. Look at the land with your own eyes, since you are not going to cross this Jordan"** (vv. 26–27). God allowed Moses to view the land from one of the highest mountains in the area. "You will see the land only from a distance; you will not enter the land I am giving to the people of Israel" (Deut. 32:52). Then He commanded Moses, **"Commission Joshua, and encourage and strengthen him, for he will lead this people across and will cause them to inherit the land that you will see"** (3:28). God would not change His mind. It was time to pass the baton of leadership to the one whom the Lord appointed to finish the mission.

●

WORDS FROM WESLEY

Deuteronomy 3:28

He shall go over—It was not Moses, but Joshua or Jesus that was to give the people rest, Heb. 4:8. 'Tis a comfort to those who love mankind, when they are dying and going off, to see God's work likely to be carried on by other hands, when they are silent in the dust. (ENOT)

DISCUSSION

Leadership has its challenges, but it is better to lead when you know where to go than to follow blindly or block a true leader's progress. Moses was a good leader in charge of many poor followers and some who got in the way.

1. What huge challenges did Moses encounter as he tried to lead the people of Israel?

2. What are challenges to pastoral leadership?

3. How can rebellion against God's appointed leaders actually be rebellion against God?

4. How can believers protect their pastor from negative criticism?

5. How did Moses and Aaron show humility in the face of negative criticism?

6. But how did Moses later show his frustration?

7. What do you learn about the character of God as you read the story of water gushing from a rock?

8. Does God make partial obedience an option? Why is it essential to fully obey whatever God commands?

9. Should Christians hold their leaders to a higher standard than Christians set for themselves? Why or why not?

PRAYER

Father, thank You for Your grace and mercy.

GOD WANTS HIS BEST FOR YOU

Deuteronomy 5:4–21

The Ten Commandments guide us as we relate to God and each other.

Why can't we drive 120 miles per hour on a city street? Why shouldn't we run red lights or fail to stop at stop signs? Why do communities have traffic laws and other laws? Shouldn't we be free to do what we want to do?

Laws were not made to be broken; they exist for our benefit. They protect us and safeguard our communities. Whoever breaks the law devalues his or her own well-being and the community's as well.

This study shows that God gave the Ten Commandments because He wanted the best for His people. He always gives His best to those who obey Him.

COMMENTARY

The Israelites had struggled through forty years of nomadic living while waiting for those wanting to return to Egypt to die. Now, finally, the children of those "unbelievers" had replaced them (Num. 26:35). This new generation had arrived on the plains of Moab (Deut. 1:5) where preparations had to be made before entering the Promised Land.

In a series of addresses, Moses included the Ten Commandments. Moses summoned all Israel and told them, "Hear, O Israel, the decrees and laws I declare in your hearing today. Learn them, and be sure to follow them" (Deut. 5:1). The Ten Commandments are unique to ancient law codes in the sense that they never state a punishment if one is disobeyed. They are direct, each beginning with "You." Not one begins with "If a man or woman . . . then" (punishment stated). They are more direct and broader in their application.

It seems God built the punishment within the infraction. Many Scriptures point to that. For example, "Your wickedness will punish you; your backsliding will rebuke you" (Jer. 2:19); and "For the waywardness of the simple will kill them, and the complacency of fools will destroy them" (Prov. 1:32).

The commandments are given in moral imperatives, not in philosophical terms. Several of them could not be prosecuted in a court of law. How could one be accused and convicted of coveting? Only God would know of the degree of guilt and exactly when the law is broken.

God First (Deut. 5:4–15)

When individuals are asked to arrange the Ten Commandments in order of importance, most will put the last five first and the first five last. They assume relationships with people are more important than a relationship with God. The Lord's arrangement demonstrates that if we get the first five in their intended place, the remainder will not be difficult to keep.

Commandment One (Deut. 5:7). The translation of the first commandment is usually rendered, **You shall have no other gods before me** (v. 7) or beside me. The original Hebrew flavor is really "in addition to me." Our danger is not leaving God for another deity. It is rather in trying to combine another deity with God. When this happens, the heart is divided. God wants to give us a unity of heart (Ezek. 11:19). It is not possible when we have two or more supreme beings vying to occupy the space meant only for the Lord.

One who permits a divided loyalty soon discovers convictions are lost in an easy tolerance. James notes that "from the same mouth come both blessing and cursing," then argues "Does a fountain send out from the same mouth both fresh and bitter water?" (3:10–11 NASB).

WORDS FROM WESLEY

Deuteronomy 5:7

I think it needful to add a few questions here, which the reader may answer between God and his own soul. *Thou shalt have none other gods before me*—Hast thou worshiped God in spirit and in truth? Hast thou proposed to thyself no end besides Him? Hath He been the end of all thy actions? Hast thou sought for any other happiness, than the knowledge and love of God? Dost thou experimentally know the only true God, and Jesus Christ whom He hath sent? Dost thou love God? Dost thou love Him with all thy heart, with all thy soul, and with all thy strength; so as to love nothing else but in that manner and degree which tends to increase thy love of Him? Hast thou found happiness in God? Is He the desire of thine eyes, the joy of thy heart? If not, thou hast other gods before Him. (ENOT)

Commandment Two (Deut. 5:8–10). While God gave the first commandment to preserve proper internal worship, the second one is to safeguard proper external worship. Seldom did God enter the world of human senses. He preferred to preserve the mystery that surrounds Him. Moses experienced God at the burning bush where God became visible by means of an angel in the fire (Ex. 3:2). God confused the Philistines with thunder (1 Sam. 7:10). To Elijah He was "a sound of gentle a blowing" (1 Kings 19:12 NASB). God knew that faith is fostered when He is surrounded by mystery.

Few people in the Western world are likely to worship a tangible god of stone; they are most likely to raise self to deity status. Any time a person thinks his or her god is one of an easy tolerance, who will allow an abridgement of any specific moral law to suit his or her own personal whim, this god then ceases to be the God of the Bible, and increasingly becomes a god of his or her own making.

Commandment Three (Deut. 5:11). Swearing by using the name of God is so common that it hardly raises any dissent. Agree with it or not, it is not possible to speak God's name in worship on Sunday, then disdain it on Monday. One may acceptably affirm, "By the help of God, I will do that!" But that affirmation is a world away from "By God, I will do that." One who makes the last statement is not invoking God's help at all. A quotation from the Dead Sea scrolls is pertinent: "He who cannot be believed without swearing is condemned already."

●

WORDS FROM WESLEY

Deuteronomy 5:11

Thou shalt not take the name of the Lord thy God in vain —Hast thou never used the name of God, unless on solemn and weighty occasions? Hast thou then used it with the deepest awe? Hast thou duly honoured His word, His ordinances, His ministers? Hast thou considered all things as they stand in relation to Him, and seen God in all? Hast thou looked upon heaven as God's throne? Upon earth as God's footstool? On every thing therein as belonging to the great king? On every creature as full of God? (ENOT)

Commandment Four (Deut. 5:12–15). In actual number of words, respect for the Lord's Day is given the greater emphasis over all the other commandments in the Bible. No small reason for it may well be that it is a commandment so easily disregarded. For one to violate this commandment is to forfeit a balance in life. We are built to allow the "fresh air" of worship to season our lives.

While a few Christians hold that the Sabbath should be on Saturday, not Sunday, the commandment does not specify Saturday, nor even the seventh day of the week, as the day of "rest." Sunday fits the requirement of the rest day after the six days of labor. For most Christians, the added event of the resurrection of Jesus on a Sunday gives greater weight to making Sunday the day for worship.

It is not possible to maintain both a memorial to the creation and a memorial to the resurrection. The Lord's Day, Sunday, is the day John indicated he was "in the Spirit" (Rev. 1:10).

God put within us a space exclusively designed for himself to occupy. Those who do not worship are never really fulfilled in life, for nothing else will satisfy His place.

Others Second (Deut. 5:16–21)

Proper relationship to God is essential for us to have a proper relationship with people. The father or mother becomes a better parent when he or she feels responsibility to God for raising the children. Anyone is more reliable at an occupation if he or she recognizes that God is overseeing all, and at the end of any day, one must answer to God for conduct.

Commandment Five (Deut. 5:16). Word order in Hebrew is important. Words placed earlier have added significance. Both here and in Exodus 20:10, *father* precedes *mother*. However, in Leviticus 19:3, the word order is reversed. Early rabbis insist that both forms were given to ensure that the same honor is to be given to both parents.

It is interesting that the word here is not *obey*. It is rather **honor** (Deut. 5:16). Paul told children, "Obey your parents in the Lord, for this is right" (Eph. 6:1), but there always comes a time when children no longer need to obey their parents. Yet, one never outgrows the need to honor parents even after they are gone.

The word *honor* in the Hebrew is frequently used when God is the object, in which case it is translated "glorify." To honor parents, then, is to accord them a respect and importance reserved for the sacred. Children who honor their parents become parents whose children in turn are more likely to honor them.

Commandment Six (Deut. 5:17). To cause the death of a human is murder—the Hebrew word here specifically means a "violent and unauthorized killing."

One must decide if the commandment is opposed to the taking of any human life at all, such as is required in capital punishment. It is clear that the Bible never considers judicial taking of a human life to violate this commandment. The apostle Paul recognized the validity of judicial punishment as he stood before the Roman official declaring his innocence. He added, "If then I am a wrongdoer and have committed anything worthy of death, I do not refuse to die" (Acts 25:11 NASB).

WORDS FROM WESLEY

Deuteronomy 5:17

Thou shalt not kill—Have you not tempted any one, to what might shorten his life? Have you tempted none to intemperance? . . . Have you done all you could in every place, to prevent intemperance of all kinds? Are you guilty of no degree of self-murder? Do you never eat or drink any thing because you like it, although you have reason to believe, it is prejudicial to your health? Have you constantly done whatever you had reason to believe was conducive to it? Have you not hated your neighbour in your heart? Have you reproved him that committed sin in your sight? If not, you have in God's account hated Him, seeing you suffered sin upon Him. Have you loved all men as your own soul? As Christ loved us? Have you done unto all men, as in like circumstances, you would they should do to you? Have you done all in your power to help your neighbours, enemies as well as friends? Have you laboured to deliver every soul you could from sin and misery? Have you shewed that you loved all men as yourself, by a constant, earnest endeavour, to fill all places with holiness and happiness, with the knowledge and love of God? (ENOT)

Since all humans were created "in the image and likeness of God," then the unauthorized taking of their life is in a sense playing God, in effect saying, "God may have brought you into this world, but I am going to take you out."

Commandment Seven (Deut. 5:18). The Bible opposes free sexual expression because of the damage it does to marriage and family. The biblical view of moral integrity is summed up in Joseph's view of illicit sex when Potiphar's wife tried to seduce him. He called it a "sin against God" (Gen. 39:90). David, at the revelation of his murder of Uriah "with the sword of the Ammonites" (2 Sam. 12:9), recognized his act a sin against God (Ps. 51:4).

The biblical view in the way God made humans is that sex says, "My completeness is in somebody else," and it is consummated for a husband and wife when they become one flesh (Gen. 2:24).

Sex outside of marriage damages individuals by causing lust and love to be confused to the point that the violators develop an inability to tell the difference between the two, ultimately eroding the ability to have complete and exclusive commitment to one mate in marriage.

Sex before marriage can cause a relationship to be based too much on sex and not enough on the delicate differences that after marriage can lead to divorce. An assessment based on how the bodies "feel" when they come together does not permit a balanced blend of personalities necessary for a marriage based on commitment.

Commandment Eight (Deut. 5:19). When a person steals something, property is elevated above people, and wholesome relationships based on trust are destroyed. Education is thwarted when a student opts to steal answers from another person. All of society has to pay in higher prices for a theft of merchandise. In effect, every robber steals from a multitude of people.

It becomes impossible to be wholesomely creative and develop initiative if those abilities are bent to "beat the system." Some employees start late and finish early, extend break periods, or loaf on the job. These should be considered stealing from an employer.

Commandment Nine (Deut. 5:20). Too often in our day, telling lies has become an acceptable form of communication.

Creditability is important to any person's acceptance and to his or her future success. Jesus said, "You will know the truth, and the truth will set you free" (John 8:32). The implication can be easily seen—lies can enslave us.

Commandment Ten (Deut. 5:17). The first commandment has to do with what one thinks and speaks against the sin of internal idolatry—having any god other than the Lord. Now we learn that the last one ends where it all began—with thoughts that harbor the sin of internal greed.

WORDS FROM WESLEY

Deuteronomy 5:21

Neither shalt thou covet any thing that is thy neighbour's—The plain meaning of this is, thou shalt not desire any thing that is not thy own, any thing which thou hast not. Indeed why shouldst thou? God hath given thee whatever tends to thy one end, holiness. Thou canst not deny it, without making Him a liar: and when any thing else will tend thereto, He will give thee that also. There is therefore no room to desire any thing which thou hast not. Thou hast already every thing that is really good for thee, wouldst thou have more money, more pleasure, more praise still? Why this is not good for thee. God has told thee so, by withholding it from thee. O give thyself up to His will and gracious disposal! (ENOT)

Covetousness is the mother of many sins because it so easily turns to other sins. It makes people turn inward, causing them to want to satisfy self at any expense. Paul informed Timothy that "people who want to get rich fall into temptation and a trap and into many foolish and harmful desires that plunge men into ruin and destruction. For the love of money is a root of all kinds of evil" (1 Tim. 6:9–10).

DISCUSSION

Good parents demand obedience from their children and therefore discipline them when they do wrong. After all, good parents want what is best for their children, and know that bad behavior leads only to trouble and failure. Our heavenly Father, too, wants only what is best for His children.

1. What might become of a society that is totally ignorant of the Ten Commandments?

2. Why is it personally satisfying to stay within the boundaries God has set for His children?

3. What was God's plan for the Israelites in giving them the Ten Commandments?

4. How might a believer be guilty of worshiping a false god; for example, money?

5. What kinds of activities often compete with the observance of a Sabbath rest and Sunday worship?

6. How would you advise young parents who asked you how they might have a happy home life?

7. Why do you agree or disagree that abortion is murder?

8. What changes would occur in your neighborhood if everyone endeavored to honor the Ten Commandments?

9. Where do evil acts originate? How does Philippians 4:8 relate to this matter?

PRAYER

Father, help us take Your commandments seriously.

10

THE OBEDIENT LIFE

Deuteronomy 6:1–12

God's Word is the guide for how to live a dedicated
Christian life in everyday activities.

Is it possible to hear without actually hearing? Of course.
Two people may hear a sermon, but one hears only words, while
the other hears with understanding and resolves to heed what
was spoken. The generation of Hebrews that was on the verge
of entering Canaan needed to hear God's commands, decrees,
and laws with understanding and resolve to obey them. Their
future depended upon how well they would hear them.

We need to teach our children and grandchildren to obey the
Word of God, but we must teach by example as well as by precept.
This study will challenge you to truly hear what God has said in
His Word.

COMMENTARY

Deuteronomy offers a series of Moses' farewell addresses to
the children of Israel. The first generation died off after refusing
to enter the Promised Land. A second generation, with little or no
memory of Egypt and meeting God at Mount Sinai, was on the
verge of taking the land.

In Deuteronomy 5, Moses repeated the Ten Commandments,
asking this generation to affirm loyalty to God and this foundational
set of instructions. "So be careful to do what the Lord your God
has commanded you; do not turn aside to the right or to the left.
Walk in all the way that the Lord your God has commanded you,
so that you may live and prosper and prolong your days in the

land that you will possess" (5:32–33). Deuteronomy 6 picks up from there.

Climbing to the Pinnacle of the Law (Deut. 6:1–3)

For the last thousands of years, Jews have considered Deuteronomy 6:4–5 the core of the Old Testament law. Early on, many faithful Jews say these words aloud to remind them of their loyalty to the one true God. If these sentences form the law's Most Holy Place, then the Ten Commandments listed in Deuteronomy 5 are just outside the heavy curtain separating the Most Holy Place from the Holy Place.

Or to change the image, the *Shema* (a Hebrew word meaning "Hear"), the title traditionally given to 6:4–5, can be seen as the highest peak in the law, and the Ten Commandments as the path of final approach to that pinnacle.

Moses began his walk through the territory between these two high points by saying, **"These are the commands, decrees and laws the Lord your God directed me to teach you"** (v. 1). With these few words, Moses began laying out the weight of the law. He did so first by using three strong words to define the content. One could draw distinctions among the three words: *commands*, *decrees*, and *laws*. Instead, Moses probably intended them to be three strokes of the same sledgehammer.

The opening sixteen words of the chapter not only answer the "what" question; they also move on to "who." Who is the source of these laws? "Yes, in one sense, I am," Moses seemed to say. "I am the herald, the messenger. If I, whom the Lord has given to guide you across the wilderness, spoke these words out of my own wisdom, they would be worthy of your attention. But these words come not merely from me. I am a messenger for the King, the Lord our God."

By this point, how many times would the people have heard Moses tell the story of God meeting him at the burning bush, or the extraordinary ways God had revealed himself as He humiliated Pharaoh, or thundered from Mount Sinai? Undoubtedly, the people could themselves tell these stories word for word. Their God had revealed himself to Moses as "I am who I AM," *Yahweh*, the word translated "LORD" in our English Bibles (Ex. 3:14). In Egypt, at the Red Sea, and at the mount, God had revealed himself to the people as their God. The commandments Moses spoke came not from himself, but from their ultimate Guide and Protector. Moses checked off the potential questions one by one: What? Who? Then, where? **In the land that you are crossing the Jordan to possess** (Deut. 6:1). What emotions would have arisen within the people as they heard these phrases? Excitement—"We will finally have a home." Fear—"We still remember our parents talking about giants who live in this land. We are not giants. How will we defeat them?" Trust—"For centuries, God has been promising to give us this land. He will not let us down. When He again demonstrates His power and grace by giving us this land, we will be so grateful. We will keep any commands God gives."

Moses finished this prologue to the *Shema* with several answers to the question why. First, why had Moses given such emphasis to the "what" and "who" of the law? So that the generation before him, as well as all succeeding generations might **fear the LORD** their **God as long as** they **live** (v. 2). Did God and Moses wish the people to live in terror before their God? No, one cannot shudder before and truly love the same being. In this context, fear implied the deepest of respect, along the same lines as one can enjoy a campfire, while at the same time respecting the dangers accompanying it. "As you think of God's law, remember who God is. Live in deepest respect for Him and for what He has instructed."

Moses moved on to a second why. Why should God's people keep God's law? To this question, Moses gave three responses. First, if you obey the law, you will live long (**so that you may**

enjoy long life [v. 2]). Those who disobeyed God's law risked God's judgment, premature death at God's own hand. In contrast, those who obeyed God's law would live at peace both with God and with each other. Second, if you obey the law, you will live well (**so that it may go well with you** [v. 3]). And third, if you obey the law, you will **increase greatly** (v. 3). God would bless His people with many children. In an agricultural society (**a land flowing with milk and honey** [v. 3]), children were an essential part of the work force.

The Pinnacle of the Law (Deut. 6:4–9)

Both 6:3 and 6:4 begin with **Hear, O Israel**. In one sense, these words are unnecessary. They add nothing to the content of what Moses said. Yet he spoke them for emphasis, just as he had emphasized the law by giving it three names (v. 1). "Pay special attention to this." When Jesus spoke centuries later in Galilee, He often punctuated His sermons with "He who has an ear, let him hear." When Jesus later spoke through John to the seven churches of Asia Minor, He encouraged them to "hear what the Spirit says to the churches."

WORDS FROM WESLEY

Deuteronomy 6:5

And thou shalt love the Lord thy God with all thine heart—And is this only an external commandment? Can any then say, that the Sinai-covenant was merely external? With all thy heart—With an entire love. He is One; therefore our hearts must be united in His love. And the whole stream of our affections must run toward Him. O that this love of God may be shed abroad in our hearts. (ENOT)

At this point, neither God nor Moses was irritated, yet they both spoke with serious intent, calling the children by name (Israel) and requesting that they listen carefully. "Listen carefully,"

Moses continued, "for there is only **one** God" (v. 4). "No competitors offer any close rivalry. He is the authority. If you do not listen to Him, there is no other upon whom you can fall back."

How should God's people respond to their God? With obedience and submission. Moses had covered this topic well in verses 1–3. God wanted obedience, but not merely so He could maintain control over His people. He knew His way was best for the people. That's why He had given the commandments to them. In covenant, He had graciously offered not only law, but He had given himself in hope of rich relationship with His people. He had revealed himself not only as the authority, but as a loving, covenant-giving Father. He who gave himself in love desired a like response. **Love the LORD your God with all your heart and with all your soul and with all your strength** (v. 5). As with the three words denoting the law, we can distinguish the meanings of the three words: *heart, soul,* and *strength*. But again, Moses and God may have used three words more for emphasis. "Don't love God lightly. Love Him with all your being, just as He offers His complete self to you."

How seriously did Moses want the people to take God's instructions? The next four verses, as it were, underline the *Shema* and the Ten Commandments that preceded them.

WORDS FROM WESLEY

Deuteronomy 6:5

What is implied in being a [holy] Christian? The loving the Lord our God with all our heart, and with all our mind, and soul, and strength (Deut. 6:5; 30:6; Ezek. 36:25–29). (WJW, vol. 8, 279)

Place **these commandments . . . upon your hearts** (v. 6). "Place them at the very core of your being. Let everything else you do and are revolve around God's law."

Impress them on your children (v. 7). We see here, within seven verses, three references to the coming generations. Moses knew the generation before him would not easily forget him or the imminent conquest of the land. But Moses also knew he would have no opportunity to speak to the next generations. He solemnly charged his hearers with responsibility for their awareness and understanding of God and His commandments.

WORDS FROM WESLEY

Deuteronomy 6:7

Father, instruct my docile heart,
Apt to instruct I then shall be,
I then shall all Thy words impart,
And teach (as taught myself by Thee)
My children in their earliest days,
To know, and live the life of grace. (PW, vol. 9, 94)

How frequently should God's people offer theological education to their children? From Moses' perspective, the better question would have been, "When should God's people *not* be offering God's truth to their children?" Perhaps only when they were asleep! **Talk about them when you sit at home and when you walk along the road, when you lie down and when you get up** (v. 7). "Let you and your children be reminded of God's law every time you hold up your hands, whenever your face is seen, whenever one is departing from or entering your house." **Tie them as symbols on your hands and bind them on your foreheads. Write them on the doorframes of your houses and on your gates** (vv. 8–9).

WORDS FROM WESLEY

Deuteronomy 6:8

Thou shalt bind them—Thou shalt give all diligence, and use all means to keep them in thy remembrance, as men often bind something upon their hands, or put it before their eyes to prevent forgetfulness of a thing which they much desire to remember. (ENOT)

A Warning Regarding the Pinnacle of the Law (Deut. 6:10–12)

The multitude standing before Moses might not easily forget the miraculous events they had experienced or the God who engineered them. But their leader had seen the previous generation doubt and disobey God even after He had single-handedly brought His people out of Egypt. So Moses warned them of a danger they themselves would not have thought possible.

"After God brings you into a home that will be unbelievably wonderful, don't take Him for granted. The land God is giving you will be so spectacular! But you will be tempted to pay more attention to the land than the One who gave you the land. How wonderful will this land be? You won't even have to build homes. You can move into **cities** that are already **large** and **flourishing**. You won't have to furnish these homes; they are already **filled with all kinds of good things** and water supplies that are well established. The perennial crops, for example the **vineyards and olive groves**, are already in place. When you sit down at your table with your well-fed families, you could **forget the LORD, who brought you out of Egypt, out of the land of slavery** (vv. 10–12). Don't let that happen!"

God promised faithful relationship with those who served Him and followed His commandments (vv. 2–3). Those who ignored Him or His instructions did so at their own peril.

DISCUSSION

Obedience is contingent on good listening. Discuss if you listen when God speaks.

1. Twice in Deuteronomy 6:1–12, Moses commanded the people of Israel to "hear." Why did he want the people of Israel to listen intently?

2. Why is it important to listen carefully to the preaching and teaching of God's Word?

3. How might a Christian improve sermon-listening skills?

4. What story did Jesus tell to stress the importance of not only hearing His words, but also doing them? How would you relate this story to modern times?

5. Generally speaking, how does consistent obedience to God contribute to one's health and longevity?

6. How well do you obey God each day? Not well at all? Half-heartedly? Wholeheartedly? In what areas of life do you still need to render wholehearted obedience?

7. According to Deuteronomy 6:7–9, where and when should a believer obey God?

8. What are some excellent ways to teach children to obey God?

9. What did God promise to give the Israelites if they obeyed Him?

10. How might life be different for a believer who decides to renounce lip service and to obey God fully?

PRAYER

Father, may we fully obey all Your commandments by fully loving You and others.

11

GOD'S PEOPLE BECAUSE OF GOD'S GRACE

Deuteronomy 8:1–18

God's people are always kept by His grace
in all situations for all times.

A little boy prayed, "Dear God, please bless Mommy and Daddy, my brother, and my baby sister, and me. And please, God, take care of yourself, because if anything happened to You, the rest of us would be in big, big trouble."

The little boy's theology was flawed, but he was partly right. Without God, we would all be in big, big trouble. We are dependent upon God for everything: our salvation, our physical well-being, our daily needs, even the air we breathe. However, just as God cared for His people throughout their desert wanderings, so He cares for us. We are blessed to be His people. His grace is incomprehensible!

This study will help you enjoy full assurance that God cares for you.

COMMENTARY

Deuteronomy is both historical and prophetical. Moses recited to the Israelites their journey out of Egypt. He also gave instructions for the future inhabitation of the Promised Land. The name *Deuteronomy* means "second law." The book was given this name because it well describes the contents. Deuteronomy is in many ways a repetition of what has been previously discussed in the first four books of the Bible.

Chapter 8 is a discourse to the Israelites on remembering the Lord and keeping His commands after they enter the Promised Land. Chapter 7 describes the Lord's favor in helping the people of Israel drive out the inhabitants of the Promised Land. The Lord promised to bless their crops, oil, herds, and flocks if they would remember His laws and commands in their new land. Chapter 9 is a reminder that the Lord did not given them this land because of their righteousness, but that by grace He was using them to overthrow the wickedness of those in the land. In chapter 9, Moses also reminded the Israelites of their tendency to worship other gods as they did the golden calf in the desert. Therefore, chapter 8 is a call to remember the Lord and His gracious acts of benevolence on their behalf to bring them to this place in life.

The Lord's Discipline (Deut. 8:1–5)

Be careful to follow every command (v. 1) is a good admonition for us today. Israel was notorious for breaking the commandment of "have no other gods before me." It is good to remember that God wants all of His commands to be obeyed, not just the ones we think are convenient. **So that** is an important phrase repeated several times in this chapter. It tells us why the previous statement has been made. Often it precedes a blessing, promise, or warning. In this passage, the phrase yields to the promise that they would **live and increase and . . . enter and possess the land** (v. 1). They would live and not be destroyed in the battle for the land. They would also live a much better quality of life than they had been experiencing for forty years in the desert. Jesus promised a better quality of life in John 10:10 when He said, "I have come that they may have life, and have it to the full." The best life is the Christian life. The inhabitation of their new land was a fulfillment of a promise from the Lord (Deut. 8:1). The Lord always keeps His promises. He is trustworthy and true. His promises bring comfort, consolation, and hope to us in our times of trial. Peter called them "great and precious promises" in 2 Peter 1:4.

The LORD your God led you all the way in the desert
(Deut. 8:2) is both a comforting and troubling thought. God leads
us through the valley of the shadow of death even as Jesus Christ
was led into the wilderness, where He endured great spiritual
warfare for forty days. We need not be troubled by the thoughts
of our heavenly Father leading us through hardship. A much
worse thought would be that we would have to lead ourselves
through it. Yet in this, God tested the Israelites to **know what
was in** their **heart** (v. 2). God can help us find purpose in the
hardships of our lives.

WORDS FROM WESLEY

Deuteronomy 8:2

It is good for us . . . to remember all the ways both of God's
providence and grace, by which He has led us hitherto through the
wilderness, that we may trust Him, and cheerfully serve Him.
(ENOT)

**He humbled you, causing you to hunger then fed you with
manna** (v. 3). The Israelites were virtually resourceless in the
desert. They were completely and totally dependent upon the
Lord for their daily sustenance. They were fed with food from
heaven, not just once, but six days a week for forty years. Manna
can still be found in the Middle East, but not the type of manna
the Israelites gathered in the desert. Although they may have
been very similar, there are several differences between the two
types. The manna in the desert did not ooze from trees; it
appeared after the morning dew. The manna in the desert was
not isolated to a certain geographical region; it went with the
Hebrew children wherever they went. Also, the heavenly manna
was not seasonal; it was constant: six days a week for forty years
excluding every Sabbath day.

In John 6:49–51, Jesus compared himself to manna, stating He is the bread that came down from heaven, the living bread, which a man shall eat and never die (live eternally). Christ quoted part of this verse when He refuted Satan during His time of temptation in Luke 4:3–4, saying, "Man does not live on bread alone." The goods and services of the world cannot satisfy the spiritual part of humanity that longs for a relationship with God. To ignore, suppress, or attempt to fill this dimension with something else are all futile efforts. Only Christ can fill the deepest longings of the human heart. The phrase **every word** (Deut. 8:3) is a good place to talk about inerrancy. We believe that the sixty-six canonical books of the Old and New Testaments are the inerrant (without error) word of God. There has not been, nor shall there ever be, "another testament" or "holy book" that follows the New Testament and is equal or superior to it.

WORDS FROM WESLEY

Deuteronomy 8:3

By every word—That is, by every or any thing which God appoints for this end, how unlikely soever it may seem to be for nourishment; seeing it is not the creature, but only God's command and blessing upon it, that makes it sufficient for the support of life. (ENOT)

Your clothes did not wear out and your feet did not swell (v. 4) are two evidences of divine intervention on their behalf. Both of these happen frequently to people who live in harsh climates without modern conveniences.

Know then in your heart (v. 5) removes any shred of doubt. More than cognitive assent, the Israelites would understand internally that **God disciplines** them (v. 5). The Hebrew term used for *discipline* comes from the root *yasar*. It means to chastise, correct, or discipline. God compares spiritual discipline to that of a father/son relationship. As a father disciplines his son, so also God disciplines His children. God's discipline is within the boundaries of covenantal relationship. God entered into a covenant with Israel at Mount Sinai, and He was remembering that commitment to them. The Israelites were disciplined, but God always provided for their every need. Additionally, God only brought such discipline upon them as was necessary for their benefit. Experiencing the discipline of God can be difficult, but it is always for our good.

A Good Land (Deut. 8:6–9)

Streams and pools of water, with springs (v. 7)—sources of water are vital for survival in the desert. The Promised Land was a place where there would be no want for water. The supply would be plentiful. This must have had significant meaning to Moses. One of the repetitive complaints of the Israelites in the desert was their yearning for water. It was a "water incident" at Meribah that precluded Moses' entrance into the Promised Land (Num. 20). It must have excited the heart of Moses to think of a land in which there would be an abundance of that which had been scarce for many years. In the New Testament, Jesus told the woman at the well that He was the source of "living water" (John 4:10). Out of Spirit-filled believers flow rivers of "living water" (John 7:38–39). Finally, flowing from the throne of heaven is a river of the water of life (Rev. 22:1).

Wheat and barley, vines and fig trees, pomegranates, olive oil and honey (Deut. 8:8)—the Promised Land would include a more varied menu than manna every day. You can imagine their delight in considering the abundance and variety of food in their new land. Many people today enjoy the harvests of crops from around the world. Other people find it difficult to feed their children each day. The promise for all is the hope of heaven and the invitation to the wedding supper of the Lamb. The Promised Land for the Israelites was so good, it was almost too good to be true.

Iron and **copper** (v. 9) could have been used for cooking utensils, mirrors, weapons, armor, plows, pruning hooks, and other items. **Out of the hills** (v. 9) expresses the easy access to these entities. Unlike their wandering in the desert and doing without, the Promised Land would have everything they needed for abundant living.

Remember the Lord (Deut. 8:10–18)

When you have eaten . . . praise the LORD (v. 10). This reminder is a good one for all who are tempted to take many aspects of their lives for granted. It is the Lord's will that we praise Him for all He has given us.

WORDS FROM WESLEY
Deuteronomy 8:10

Bless the Lord—Solemnly praise Him for thy food; which is a debt both of gratitude and justice, because it is from His providence and favour that thou receivest both thy food and refreshment and strength by it. The more unworthy and absurd is that too common profaneness of them, who, professing to believe a God, from whom all their comforts come, grudge to own Him at their meals, either by desiring His blessing before them, or by offering due praise to God after them. (ENOT)

The predominant idea in this section is simply this: Remember the Lord in your prosperity, for it was He and not yourselves who bestowed all this goodness upon you. Moses said to **be careful** not to **forget** Him, **otherwise your heart will become proud** (vv. 11–12, 14). He reminded them that God delivered them from the **venomous snakes and scorpions** and **brought . . . water out of hard rock** (v. 15). It was the Lord who provided **manna** (v. 16) and who gave the courage and strength to posses this land. Be careful to **remember the LORD** (v. 18) in your prosperity. Psalm 100 mentions something similar when it says in verse 3 that it is God who has made us and not we ourselves. "We are his people."

Commands . . . laws . . . decrees (Deut. 8:11)—these terms encompass everything the Israelites knew about the Lord and His expectations for them. A similar admonition is given in Philippians 3:16: "Only let us live up to what we have already attained."

Eat and are satisfied (Deut. 8:12)—no more manna but an abundance and variety of foods.

Build fine houses—they would be rid of their tents; they could **settle down** (v. 12).

All you have is multiplied (v. 13)—divine discipline was to be followed by divine blessing in every area of their lives.

Your heart will become proud and you will forget the LORD (v. 14). One of the great tragedies in Christendom is when God transforms and blesses a person, only to be forgotten. There is a lot of truth to Charles Spurgeon's statement that the great test of believers is not poverty but prosperity. Both history and the New Testament support that thought in recording the luxurious and licentious behavior of the Roman Empire. Jesus made several comments on faith and finances. In Mark 10:21, Christ told the rich young ruler to sell all he had and follow Him. In the Sermon on the Mount, Jesus taught the disciples to lay up treasures in heaven, "For where your treasure is, there your heart will be also" (Matt. 6:21).

Desert . . . snakes . . . scorpions (Deut. 8:15)—it was only by the grace of God that Israel survived their experience in the wilderness. By grace they became the people of God. By grace they experienced the prosperity of God. By grace they remained His chosen people. Similarly, "For it is by grace you have been saved, through faith—and this not from yourselves, it is the gift of God—not by works, so that no one can boast" (Eph. 2:8–9).

Moses, at the Lord's command, made a bronze snake and put it on a pole. Everyone who was bitten and looked to the bronze snake lived (Num. 21). Similarly, when Jesus Christ is lifted up, those who look to Him are saved (John 12:32).

WORDS FROM WESLEY

Deuteronomy 8:16

That he might humble thee—By keeping thee in a constant dependence upon Him for every day's food, and convincing thee what an impotent, helpless creature thou art, having nothing whereon to subsist, and being supported wholly by the alms of divine goodness from day to day. The mercies of God, if duly considered, are as powerful a mean to humble us as the greatest afflictions, because they increase our debts to God, and manifest our dependence upon Him, and by making God great, they make us little in our own eyes. *To do thee good*—That is, that after He hath purged and prepared thee by afflictions, thou mayest receive and enjoy His blessings with less disadvantage, whilst by the remembrance of former afflictions thou art made thankful for them, and more cautious not to abuse them. (ENOT)

My power . . . my hands (Deut. 8:17)—there are no self-made people. It is God who enables us with various gifts and talents from His Holy Spirit.

The ability to produce wealth (v. 18) comes from God and Him alone. It was for the Israelites a confirmation of **his covenant** with them.

DISCUSSION

"Amazing Grace" is often played at funerals, but we should reflect upon God's grace at happy times too. His grace is with us all the time.

1. What is the biggest difference between punishment and discipline?

2. What was God's purpose in Israel's desert wanderings?

3. How did God's grace turn a negative experience in your life to a positive experience?

4. Have you experienced God's discipline? If so, how does God reveal His love in the discipline?

5. How does God demonstrate His trustworthiness every day?

6. Do you agree or disagree that we need God's grace to serve Him faithfully?

7. How does grace counter the notion that we deserve God's blessings?

8. How does recalling God's past goodness help us rely on His grace today and in the future?

9. How might a Christian show that he or she appreciates God's grace?

PRAYER

Father, help us cling to You during prosperity as we do in adversity.

12

GIVING: THE WORSHIP EXPERIENCE

Deuteronomy 26:1–19

Only giving our best to God is worthy to be called worship.

Worship includes far more than singing praise choruses or hymns. Our giving should be an act of worship. We show by our giving that we acknowledge God as the Giver of all we have. We dedicate our offerings and ourselves to Him as an act of worship, and we contemplate the grace by which He allows us to be faithful stewards of all He entrusts to us.

God directed the Hebrews to worship Him with firstfruits when they entered Canaan. He also instructed them to give tithes and offerings. Such presentations to God were appropriate expressions of the Hebrews' covenant relationship with God.

This study will challenge you, as one of God's children, to worship Him through faithful giving.

COMMENTARY

Deuteronomy 26 marks the conclusion of a rehearsal by Moses of some of the laws given in Exodus and Leviticus. He began this legislative section of the book in 12:1 with the words, "These are the decrees and laws you must be careful to follow in the land that the LORD, the God of your fathers, has given you to possess." He concludes in 26:16 with, "The LORD your God commands you this day to follow these decrees and laws." Between these two verses are found laws that relate primarily to the ordinary Hebrew, laws giving direction in practical day-to-day living issues. They are the laws and decrees they would need to know and follow if they were to please God in this new land.

Chapter 26 divides naturally into three sections. The first section (vv. 1–11) describes the appropriate ritual required in offering the firstfruits of the land. The second section (vv. 12–15) shares the procedure and confession associated with the triennial offering. The last section (vv. 16–19) pictures a beautiful wedding ceremony between God and His people.

The Offering of the Firstfruits (Deut. 26:1–11)

This section contains the details of the liturgy required in presenting the firstfruits of the land. There is no indication that this was to be an annual ritual in connection with the offering described in Exodus 23:16–19. Considering the form of the liturgy, it seems most likely that this particular offering was to be made at the end of the first harvest season. It is striking in both its simplicity and significance. The presenter is reminded of God's gracious provision in the past and present. He was called upon to confess his dependence on God and to share God's blessings with others.

The Presentation (Deut. 26:1–2). **When you have entered the land the LORD your God is giving you** (v. 1). Three things should be noted from this opening verse. First, the presentation of the firstfruits would not and could not occur until they had entered the land. The firstfruits would be the product of their residency. While travelling from Egypt, they were not farmers; they did not till the land. God supplied water, bread, and meat for their journey (Ex. 15:25; 16:4, 11). In the land of their inheritance, when they had **taken possession of it and settled in it** (Deut. 26:1), they would become an agricultural society and only then could they bring the offering of the firstfruits of the land. Second, they are reminded that this is the land that God was about to give them. They didn't own it, they hadn't worked for it, and they didn't deserve it. God was going to freely give it to them. Third, He is their God. He is not any of the gods of the land. He is not any of the gods of Egypt. He is the one and only Lord God Jehovah to whom they owed their life and their all.

Following their first harvest in this new land, they were to **take some of the firstfruits of all** of the **produce from the soil of the land . . . and put them in a basket** (v. 2). The firstfruits of the harvest were to be offered at the Feast of Weeks (Deut. 16:9–12; Ex. 34:22–26). This offering acknowledged that it was God who provided all just as He always had done. Although similar to the Feast of Weeks offering and perhaps offered at the same time, the ritual here described seems to be confined to the first offering in the new land. We should not miss the striking contrast between all God had given and the basket with **some of the firstfruits** (Deut. 26:2). But again the Israelites were reminded that it came from the soil of the land God had given them. Considering the battles they would fight to drive out the occupants of the land, it would have been easy for them to think they had taken the land themselves. That is why this simple act of worship was so important, for at harvest time they would be reminded of God's goodness and blessing. God who had delivered and had provided throughout their history would continue to supply their needs in the Promised Land. Not only must they take some of the firstfruits and put them in a basket, but they must also make the offering at **the place the LORD their God** would **choose** (v. 2). This further act of obedience kept God at the center of the entire time of celebration. He would and had come to them many times, but this time they were to come to Him.

The Act of Worship and Confession (Deut. 26:3–10). Interestingly, the first act of confession is to **the priest in office at the time** (v. 3), that is, the priest on duty in the sanctuary when the offering of the firstfruits is brought. In prescribed Old Testament pattern, the approach to God is through the priest. To the priest one would confess, **"I declare today to the LORD your God that I have come to the land the LORD swore to our forefathers to give us."** It is only as one acknowledged openly that the land wherein he now resided was given by God and that he was an heir of a promise made long ago to his forefathers that he was permitted to address God himself. Once this simple confession was made, then, on behalf of God, the **priest** took **the basket** and placed it **in front of the altar** (v. 4).

Following this act of worship and confession, the presenter is directed to recite a more complete and descriptive acknowledgment of God's blessing, deliverance, and provision. He is directed to first recall that his **father was a wandering Aramean** (v. 5). There is no doubt that the reference is to Jacob, who spent considerable time in Aramea working for Laban, his father-in-law, and who married two Aramean women. Although Jacob had twelve sons, his family was relatively small when **he went down into Egypt with a few people and lived there and became a great nation, powerful and numerous** (v. 5). The significance of this confession is to acknowledge God's great blessing on his forefathers. The few and seemingly insignificant desert wanderers became powerful and numerous. In verses 6–8, our presenter is called upon to remember and confess God's gracious deliverance from Egypt and bondage. This is a recurring theme throughout the Old Testament from Exodus to Malachi. Israel was never to forget what God had done for them in setting them free and here. As they brought the firstfruits of the land God had given them, they did so in the context of God's longstanding and loving care for His people. In addition to the symbolic offering of the firstfruits in the basket, the presenter was to fully acknowledge that it had all come from God. It was God who had **brought** them **to this place** and had given them **this land, a land flowing with milk and honey** (v. 9).

Sharing the Blessing (Deut. 26:11). Although it has been acknowledged through this ritual that all of the increase of the land is attributable to God's blessing, only a small portion has actually been brought to the sanctuary. The basket is representative of the whole. Now God reminded the one presenting the offering that there were others who were less fortunate and with whom he must share. These are **the Levites and the aliens** (v. 11) who also live in the land but who have no actual inheritance; because of God's blessing and the generosity of God's people, they too would have cause to rejoice.

WORDS FROM WESLEY

Deuteronomy 26:11

Thou shalt rejoice—Thou shalt hereby be enabled to take comfort in all thy employments, when thou hast sanctified them by giving God His portion, it is the will of God, that we should be cheerful not only in our attendance upon His holy ordinances, but in our enjoyment of the gifts of His providence. Whatever good thing God gives us, we should make the most comfortable use of it we can, still tracing the streams to the fountain of all consolation. (ENOT)

The Triennial Tithe (Deut. 26:12–15)

It was made clear to the Israelites in Leviticus 27:30 that "a tithe of everything from the land . . . belongs to the LORD." However, once every three years (skipping the sabbatical year) a special tithe was to be taken that was to provide for the needs of "the Levites (who have no allotment or inheritance of their own) and the aliens, the fatherless and the widows" (Deut. 14:29). Here in 26:12–15, Moses shared a liturgy that was to accompany this offering. Generosity to the less fortunate was central to this offering. The command is clear: **When you have finished setting aside a tenth of all your produce in the third year, the year of the tithe, you shall give** (v. 12). There is a time when the setting aside is to be completed and it is to be a tenth of *all* of the produce. Then all of the tenth is to be given **to the Levite,**

the alien, the fatherless and the widow, that they too may **be satisfied** (v. 12).

To further impress on the Israelites the significance of this offering, God instituted the liturgy outlined in verses 13–15. This liturgy is a declaration by the one distributing the tithe that he acted with honesty, integrity, and in obedience to God's command. Verse 13 is a personal profession that all that was supposed to be done was done. The one offering the tithe must affirm, **"I have not turned aside from your commands nor have I forgotten any of them."** As the liturgy continues, his confession moved from the general to the specific. **"I have not eaten any of the sacred portion while I was in mourning"** (v. 14) perhaps refers to removing it from his house while ceremonially unclean during the period of mourning; **"nor have I offered any of it to the dead"** (v. 14) possibly refers to offering a portion to an idol on behalf of the dead, a custom of other religions at that time. In all he had done, he could confidently say, **"I have obeyed the LORD my God; I have done everything you commanded me"** (v. 14)—not in pride but in humble confidence that he had been obedient to God, who had blessed him and had given him this **land flowing with milk and honey** (v. 15).

WORDS FROM WESLEY

Deuteronomy 26:15

Look down—After that solemn profession of their obedience to God's commands, they are taught to pray for God's blessing. (ENOT)

The Bride and the Bridegroom (Deut. 26:16–19)

With the closing verses of this chapter, Moses concluded his recital of the laws he began in chapter 12. At this point, Moses' tone changed as he shared very personally and intimately the relationship between God and His people: **"You have declared this day ... and the LORD has declared this day ..."** (vv. 17–18). One cannot help but think of a bride and bridegroom sharing vows at an altar. Here the bride, God's chosen people, pledged allegiance to Him and Him alone (v. 17). In response, the Bridegroom affirms His love and the depth of the relationship between himself and His bride (vv. 18–19). His bride is **his treasured possession** (v. 18), and He will set it **in praise, fame and honor** as **a people holy to the LORD** (v. 19). The expression "treasured possession" is first used by God in Exodus 19:5 as He talked with Moses on Mount Sinai as He began to flesh out the covenant relationship between himself and His own. How significant and personal a relationship—to be God's treasured possession and to be exalted before all the nations! That God should choose them to be His very own people is in itself an overwhelming expression of praise, fame, and honor. However, God goes far beyond that in providing for their needs and the needs of all who would dwell in this Promised Land. All He asked in return is their loving obedience to His commands, commands that are ultimately for their good.

WORDS FROM WESLEY

Deuteronomy 26:18

Avouched thee—Hath owned thee for such before all the world by eminent and glorious manifestations of His power and favour, by a solemn entering into covenant with thee, and giving peculiar laws, promises, and privileges to thee above all mankind. (ENOT)

DISCUSSION

A cynical person may accuse churches of being interested only in money, but a believer who loves the Lord delights to participate in the church offering. Discuss why this is.

1. The term *firstfruits* means more than simply first crops. What else does it mean?

2. Why should a believer give his or her best to the Lord?

3. Should a believer tithe or give more than a tithe? Defend your answer.

4. How can faithful giving be an act of worship?

5. If a believer cannot give joyfully, should he or she still give? Why or why not?

6. What ministries of compassion do you believe are worthy of your support? How might a church reach people for Christ by ministering to the material needs of the poor?

7. Believers should not give to the Lord's work to buy the Lord's blessings, but when they give generously, faithfully, joyfully, and from a loving heart, what blessings do you think the Lord will shower upon them?

8. When have you seen God's people give far beyond anyone's expectation? What, do you think, prompted such generosity?

9. Do you think Christians should give financial support to a parachurch ministry if they do not give at least a tithe to their church? Why or why not?

10. How would you respond to a church member who says it is wise to keep the pastor poor so he or she will stay humble and dependent on the Lord?

PRAYER

Father, thank You for Your abundant blessings to us.

13

HOW TO MAKE RIGHT CHOICES

Deuteronomy 29:1–4; 30:5–20

Choose life.

Choices have consequences. If we choose to follow a diet of healthful food, we can expect to enjoy good health. If we choose to follow a diet of junk food, we can expect to suffer ill health. If we choose to sleep on the job, we will most likely get fired. If we work diligently, we will most likely get rewarded.

God informed His people in the desert that He was setting clear choices before them. Good things would result if they chose to obey Him. Bad things would result if they chose to disobey Him. In all of life's choices, the best one is to obey God. This study will persuade you to make that choice daily.

COMMENTARY

Our reading finds Moses encamped with God's people near Mount Nebo at Beth Peor on the border of Canaan, in anticipation of conquering this long-Promised Land. Forty years earlier, God's people were prevented from entering Canaan by their sin and rebellion.

Now, God led His people a second time to Canaan's border, commanding Moses to summon the people to be challenged again by God's covenant originally made at Mount Sinai. It would be this new generation's responsibility to embrace or reject God's provisions and expectations (Deut. 29:1).

Covenants were quite influential in the Old Testament. The Hebrew phrase "to make a covenant" (*karat berit*) meant literally to "cut a covenant." To enter an agreement, animals were slaughtered, then cut in half with the pieces laid opposite each other, leaving a pathway between them. Those entering into the agreement would walk between the pieces while making an oath that they would become like the carcasses if they broke the covenant (see Gen. 15:7–19).

Archeology has enlightened us regarding covenant forms in the Middle East. God used a style resembling a Suzerainty Treaty, normally made between a king and his subjects. It had four main parts: the preamble presented the king's name, titles, and so forth. The prologue listed the king's prior acts of kindness toward the people. This was a way of reminding the people that they should be grateful for what they had received. The stipulation section was a detailed list of the king's expectations for his subjects. The final section listed the sanctions detailing what would happen if the people failed to adhere to the agreement. These different sections can be found in the covenant God was calling the Israelites to embrace (Deut. 29) as follows: prologue (vv. 2–8), stipulation (vv. 9–18), and sanctions (vv. 19–29). There is no preamble included, no doubt because the people were already aware that God was the source of this agreement.

The sanctions listed against Israel have a major influence in our reading. The list was more than a warning; it was prophetic, as it detailed the actual experience that happened to Israel during its captivity period. Associated with these sanctions is a gracious addition found in Deuteronomy 30:1–10. This addition describes a second chance for Israel, even if they broke the original covenant and suffered God's sanctions. Their destruction would not be final. They could be restored if they turned back to God with a whole heart. Nehemiah would remind God of this promise when he interceded for Jerusalem at the close of the Babylonian exile (Neh. 1:8–9).

Moses Summoned All the Israelites (Deut. 29:1–4)

Obedient to God, Moses summoned an audience made up of several distinct groups. The overall gathering was the nation of Israel. These people were on the edge of a blessing, even though God had not yet enlightened their minds to everything (v. 4). A subgroup within this nation was those forty-one to fifty-nine years of age who had come out of Egypt with Moses forty years earlier. Many could remember much of what God had done in their miraculous release and the original encounter at Sinai. A second subgroup was made up of those who were born during the wanderings, and only knew life as a nomad. Finally, there was each person as an individual, for the covenant applied individually as well as corporately.

WORDS FROM WESLEY

Deuteronomy 29:1

These are the terms or conditions upon which God hath made, that is, renewed His covenant with you. The covenant was but one in substance, but various in the time and manner of its dispensation. (ENOT)

Moses began his challenge by sharing a prologue, claiming his hearers had seen all that the Lord had done to Pharaoh and his officials in Egypt. Where technically only a portion of these people actually witnessed the events, doubtless the experiences were retold around numerous campfires during their forty years of wandering. Thus, experience and faith come together with the challenge from God to remember and believe. Even if they were not completely aware of His will for them in the future (v. 4), they could be reassured by their experiences from the past.

The Lord Your God Will Bring You Back (Deut. 30:5)

Our reading now jumps to the other end of God's covenant, picking up where He shared His second-chance option with the people. If Israel found itself suffering the consequences of their disobedience, they could still find deliverance if they were willing to turn back to Him. This return to God is described in three parts: (1) when they take God's covenant to heart; (2) when they return to Him; and (3) when they commit to obeying Him with all their heart and soul. Once these three criteria were met, God would restore them. The promise remains true today for everyone. If we take our relationship with Him seriously, repent of (turn away from) our sins, and commit ourselves to holy living, God will once again restore us, both as individuals and as a nation (2 Chron. 7:13–14).

In this bilateral agreement, if Israel would be sincere in their return to God, He promised to respond in four ways. Each response is introduced by the same repetitive phrase, "The LORD your God will . . ." (Deut. 29:3). The English translation deprives us of a full appreciation of this phrase. The original Hebrew literally states, "Yahweh your God will . . ." Yahweh is the name God used to describe himself to Moses at the burning-bush experience (Ex. 3:12–15). The English makes generic what the Hebrew makes specific. Yahweh, not any other deity, would deliver them.

WORDS FROM WESLEY

Deuteronomy 29:4

Yet the Lord—That is, you have perceived and seen them with the eyes of your body, but not with your minds and hearts; you have not yet learned rightly to understand the word and works of God, so as to know them for your good, and to make a right use of them, and to comply with them. . . . God's readiness to do us good in other things, is a plain evidence, that if we have not grace, that best of gifts, 'tis our own fault and not His. (ENOT)

In Moses' day, gods were said to live within geographical and political boundaries. The area of their influence was normally confined to the land and among the people who worshiped them. To be removed to a foreign land was more than geography; it was theology, because it brought individuals under the influence of a foreign god, separating them from the deity left behind. This was the lament of the psalmist who wrote of the ridicule received from Israel's captors (Ps. 137:1–4). Jonah thought he could escape God by fleeing to Tarshish (Jon. 1:1–3). But Yahweh promised that no distance or deity could prevent His rescue of those who desire a relationship with Him. Even if the people were "banished to the most distant land under the heavens" (v. 4), Yahweh would bring them back. Despite their understanding, God's presence is universal. Jonah learned this in the teeth of a storm and the belly of a sea creature. The psalmist realized there is no place, real or figurative, that one can go to be free from Yahweh's presence (Ps. 139:7–10). We may not consider our separation from God geographically, but sin can make us feel quite distant from Him. But there is no influence of sin so great that God cannot deliver us, if we sincerely desire Him.

The Lord Your God Will Circumcise Your Hearts (Deut. 30:6–7)

Circumcision was introduced to Abraham by God as a mark of participation in His covenant (Gen. 17:1–14). In circumcision, the removal of the foreskin was a statement that if the person broke God's covenant, they would also be cut off from God and separated from His people. However, rebellion against God is not an external issue, but an internal one. Commitments can be symbolized, but what makes the person different is what happens inwardly (Rom. 2:28). If Israel was sincere in her return, God would change her inner nature, giving the people the ability to live for Him. The mark of God's covenant would be found in the inner person, not the outward appearance. This is God's promised work today on the fallen nature of humankind, which transforms us from sinner to saint, so we can live without rebellion against Him.

WORDS FROM WESLEY

Deuteronomy 30:6

For the Lord will circumcise thine heart, will by His word and spirit change and purge thy heart from all thine idolatry and wickedness, and incline thy heart to love Him. God will first convert and sanctify them, the fruit whereof shall be, that they shall return and obey God's commandments. (ENOT)

The Lord Your God Will Put All These Curses on Your Enemies (Deut. 30:7–9)

In relationship to curses, a word spoken was more than a sound; it became an extension of the person who uttered it. The power of the word was found in the soul who spoke it. Thus a curse could inflict harm. Israel's disobedience would result in God inflicting a curse upon them. But to return to God would result in the making of these curses into a defense against those who were against them. This was a foundational promise expressed first when God originally called Abraham to follow Him (Gen. 12:3).

The removal of sin's negative effect can deliver us from self-inflicted curses. Decisions and actions can leave us with residual influences that plague our lives. Many suffer lives of self-created curses that they endure daily. God promises to deliver us from these and give us peace (John 14:27; Matt. 11:28–30).

The Lord Your God Will Make You Most Prosperous (Deut. 30:9–11)

Prosperity and wealth have always been understood as a sign of God's blessing. God promised this prosperity in four areas of Israel's experience: industry (work of their hands), procreation, herds, and harvest. Each of these was extremely important for survival. This should not be confused as a "prosperity religion." It is not that God will make one rich, but that He will remove from our daily existence the empty fruitlessness of life. Our efforts will no longer be futile but fulfilling. We will once again enjoy purpose in our life.

What I Am Commanding You Today Is Not too Difficult (Deut. 30:11–14)

God promised Israel three things regarding His covenant: (1) It is possible for them to fulfill; (2) it is not something beyond their grasp; and (3) it is something that indwells them. Too often our first response to God's call of obedience is to write it off as impossible. Israel was no different. They were willing to make commitments verbally that would falter in practice. But God's will can be done. He provides all we need to be faithful to Him. He removes our distance from Him, changes our rebellious nature, protects us from our enemies, and provides for our prosperity. The key word is *obedience*. But despite what we think, all things are possible with God, even our salvation.

●

WORDS FROM WESLEY
Deuteronomy 30:14

In thy mouth—Thou knowest it so well, that it is the matter of thy common discourse. *In thy heart*—In thy mind (as the heart is very commonly taken), to understand and believe it. In a word, the law is plain and easy: but the gospel is much more so. (ENOT)

Now I Set before You Today Life (Deut. 30:15–20)

God brought His covenant to a close by challenging His people to choose either life or death; be obedient or cursed. The same options are made available as were presented to Adam and

Eve. They could choose which tree to eat from, the Tree of Life or the Tree of Knowledge of Good and Evil. The former provided life; the latter resulted in death (Gen. 2:9, 16–17). It is this very death God is calling His people to turn away from to embrace His life. As it was true then, it is true today. God's great desire is that we will all choose life (2 Pet. 3:9).

WORDS FROM WESLEY

Deuteronomy 30:19

Chose life—They shall have life that chose it: they that chose the favour of God, and communion with Him, shall have what they chose. They that come short of life and happiness, must thank themselves only. They had had them, if they had chosen them, when they were put to their choice: but they die, because they will die. (ENOT)

DISCUSSION

No one plans to fail, but many people fail to plan. Nothing is more important than planning to spend eternity with the Lord.

1. Why did Moses gather the people of Israel together in Moab?

2. What was the best choice you ever made? Why was it such a good choice?

3. Why would circumcision of the heart be far more important than circumcision of the flesh in the lives of the people of Israel? Why are outward symbols of religion worthless without a cleansed heart?

4. God promised to prosper Israel if the nation would keep His commands and decrees. What is your opinion of the prosperity gospel that is often proclaimed today? Why do you hold that opinion?

5. God told the Israelites that His commands were not too difficult to understand. Why do you agree or disagree that it is not too hard to understand God's will today?

6. How has God set before people today a clear choice between life and death?

7. Romans 6:23 clearly defines "the wages of sin" as "death." What kind of death is this?

8. What can you do to help the lost choose life?

9. Israel rejected Jesus, the Messiah, but does the future hold restoration for Israel? Why or why not?

PRAYER

Father, may we love You, listen to Your voice, and hold fast to You.

WORDS FROM WESLEY WORKS CITED

ENOT: Wesley, J. (1765). *Explanatory Notes upon the Old Testament* (Vol. 1–3). Bristol: William Pine.

PW: *The Poetical Works of John and Charles Wesley.* Edited by D. D. G. Osborn. 13 vols. London: Wesleyan-Methodist Conference Office, 1868.

WJW: *The Works of John Wesley.* Third Edition, Complete and Unabridged. 14 vols. London: Wesleyan Methodist Book Room, 1872.

OTHER BOOKS IN THE
WESLEY BIBLE STUDIES SERIES

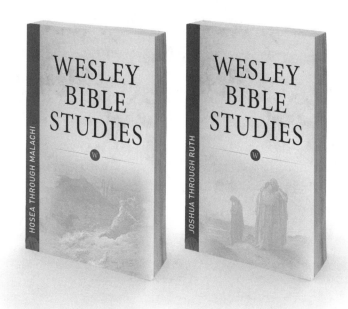

The <u>Wesley Bible</u> is unique in that it is <u>NOT</u> a new translation. Rather, it is the classic King James Bible, with some modernization of the language, ~~and~~ combined with use of alternative words used in other translations, which are provided in parentheses, when these alternative terms shed light upon the possible meanings of a given passage.